The Split Self
from Goethe to Broch

Other books by PETER B. WALDECK:

Die Kindheitsproblematik bei Hermann Broch

Perspectives on "Hamlet" (coeditor with William G. Holzberger)

The Split Self

from Goethe to Broch

Peter B. Waldeck

Lewisburg
Bucknell University Press

London: Associated University Presses

Associated University Presses, Inc.
Cranbury, New Jersey 08512

Associated University Presses
Magdalen House
136– 148 Tooley Street
London SE1 2TT, England

Library of Congress Cataloging in Publication Data

Waldeck, Peter Bruce.
    The split self.

    Bibliography: p.
    Includes index.
    1. German literature—History and criticism—
Addresses, essays, lectures. 2. Split self in
literature—Addresses, essays, lectures. I. Title.
PT148.S73W3   1979   830′.9   77-92576
ISBN 0-8387-2214-8

PRINTED IN THE UNITED STATES OF AMERICA

Respectfully dedicated to

WOLFGANG PAULSEN

Contents

Preface

THE purpose of this study is not primarily to examine the theme of the split self for its own sake, but to interpret a number of individual works. These are not interpretations in a comprehensive sense; rather they are analyses of a poetic device of central, form-generating significance. I had originally intended the individual chapters to be largely independent of one another, so that the theme of the split self as an abstraction would not overshadow or discolor the works as unique products of a personality and a historical context. However, in the course of my investigation I discovered that the poets usually left evidence pointing to one or more of the earlier treatments of the theme and that these lines of influence demanded closer scrutiny than I had anticipated. The theme of the split self, as such, therefore assumed greater significance than I had expected. But this emphasis is justified to the extent that it can be shown to have existed historically in the consciousness of the various poets. Despite this necessary shift of emphasis I have tried to maintain the integrity and independence of the individual analyses, so that the reader interested in a specific work will find the relevant chapter intelligible in itself.

My interest in the split-self theme began in 1966 when, as a graduate student at the University of Connecticut, I noticed it in Hermann Broch's *Die Schlafwandler* and subsequently developed it in my dissertation, *Die Kindheitsproblematik bei Hermann Broch.*[1] Since then, in the course of following the theme through the other authors discussed here, I have found varying degrees of recognition of a split self in the literature on a number of the works; it is quite prominent in Kafka, less prominent in Goethe, and completely overlooked in some others. But even where the theme has been noticed, it has either not been defined in the most satisfactory manner (as I see it) or has simply been left without any real analysis or any attempt to demonstrate its unifying function in the structure of the work. Chiefly Walter Sokel, in his Kafka book (and following him a number of other Kafka scholars), and perhaps Ilse Graham, in her interpretation of *Götz*, have treated it in the depth it calls for. But in these cases I found myself—with reluctance and discomfort—disagreeing with their analyses on one point or another. I regret the appearance of engaging these fine and admired scholars in polemics, and I hope that differences in viewpoint will not obscure my debt to them. Above all, it is a pleasure and something of a relief to encounter similar or related points of view in the Babel of contemporary literary criticism.

This raises the question of critical methodology—a matter that must be touched upon, even at the risk of raising disagreement of a fundamental nature. In general I subscribe to Jost Hermand's argument, in *Synthetisches Interpretieren*, that we must, as students of literature, open ourselves to all points of view—philosophical, psychological, sociological, biographical, rhetorical, and so on, that may be relevant to a given text. Consequently, in principle we must recognize ourselves as amateurs, rather than clinging to a narrow focus of what we imagine to be *Literaturwissenschaft*.

The Anglo-Saxon criticism, in particular, has never been troubled by the rigidities and the glaucoma that result from this unfortunate term. This is not to open the doors to total subjectivism and irresponsibility. Nevertheless, in principle it tends to replace a linguistic laboratory with the denser landscape of associations and significances that accompany the printed page yet cannot be pinned down to it. I am not sure that I have actually proceeded in the manner Hermand has in mind, particularly in view of the essentially psychological focus of this study. But I think an important implication of his reasoning, intended or not, is that literature must be acknowledged as something nonphysical, arising from the printed page in a subtle *Gestalt*, just as the processes of mind are not identical with the physical structure of the brain. Literature is not solely a matter of what is rationally formulated or explicitly manifested in a text. Radiating from this core is an aura of ideas, emotions, conscious and unconscious reflections of sources and traditions, personal significances for the poet, all of which constitute the experience of the art work. It is my hope to suggest a small part of this, with more confidence in some cases, less in others. Accordingly, I have indulged in some speculations and resisted or deleted others that I felt crossed a certain threshold into the probably false. The burden must lie upon the reader to add his critical judgment and sensibility to this process, to accept or reject arguments and trains of thought—not, perhaps, from the simple reasoning that "this is not proved," but from a more holistic critical response that what is being suggested is fruitful or pointless, that light is being shed on the work or that it is being obscured by sterile terminology. No doubt, the informed reader will also find clear and indisputable errors in this study, but I can only hope that they will not be so numerous or fundamental as to nullify the attempt to make a useful contribution to our appreciation of the works under discussion.

Generally, I have tried in the case of each author to focus on a single work, with a look backward at his possible and probable sources and forward to echoes of the theme in his later works (or in the work of a following author, as in the case of Walter Hasenclever). By this means I have attempted to embed the analysis of each work in a meaningful personal and historical context, even if occasionally on the basis of uncertain evidence. My objective was to provide as solid a foundation as I could for the less tangible, emotional values and relationships that gather around every interpretation. In this way, I hoped I might fairly reflect the meaning of the work for the poet and merit the reader's participation.

Despite the view, implicit here, that the poet and his work are a unity, I have kept the discussion of the lives of the poets to a minimum, for two reasons. First, I have attempted to avoid a substitution of biography for interpretation. The focus of this study is on the work itself, and I have generally restricted biographical side-glances at the lives of the poets to the barest essentials, so as not to dilute this focus and risk attributing to the poet within the work characteristics and significances applicable to him only outside of it. The exception is Goethe, whose *Götz* is not a closed circle superimposed upon the larger, if less organized, background of his life, but an open figure extended and completed by his life. The text of *Götz* does not contain within itself all the information and relationships necessary to understand its significance as an autobiographical expression. *Götz*, on one level, is a statement by and for Goethe, a self-realization to be appreciated and shared vicariously by the public, but only to the extent that it is willing to accept and probe the subjectivity of its author. Second, I have wished to avoid filling out my text with gratuitous biographical accounts, copied or condensed from various detailed treatments of individual authors. The relatively narrow focus of this study justifies, I think, this somewhat austere approach. The purpose of acquainting oneself with the lives of the authors is more properly fulfilled by consulting biographical studies.

I have attempted to deal with the difficult and problematic issue of translation of quotations by providing the bulk of the original German in the text, with English in notes. Individual words and phrases, integrated into my English text, are generally provided in English only. With this procedure I hope (a) to preserve the substance of original quotation necessary for *Germanisten;* (b) to make the text practically accessible to a possible wider audience unfamiliar with German; and (c) to eliminate the unesthetic shifting back and forth between languages in the flow of my text. While this procedure runs the risk of alienating the scholarly reader who may feel that *all* quotations should be in the original, I am also mindful that the current disinterest in psychological approaches to literature in Germany helps to justify the attempt to accommodate a wider readership.

Notes

1. Peter B. Waldeck, *Die Kindheitsproblematik bei Hermann Broch* (Munich: Wilhelm Fink Verlag, 1968).

Acknowledgments

I wish to thank Suhrkamp Verlag, Frankfurt am Main, for permission to quote from Hermann Broch, *Gesammelte Werke*, vol. 2, *Die Schlafwandler* (original copyright Rhein-Verlag, Zurich, 1931/32).

I am also grateful to the American Council of Learned Societies, Bucknell University, and Susquehanna University for financial support.

Special gratitude is due my wife, Rita, for correcting my grammar and putting up with my evil disposition while writing.

Introduction

I

Turning to the split-self theme, we must first place the present concept in a meaningful context. The split self in its broadest sense is universal in literature, yet at the same time only spottily acknowledged in literary criticism. When Balzac boasted of having worlds within him waiting to be realized, he was expressing one extreme of the universal Creator-self of the poet in his work—namely, a complete identification or absorption of his self in his creation, in which his Creator's hand binds all his figures simply by virtue of their emanation from him. But a unity at this level has no immediate critical significance for interpretation. More specifically, Freud observed that the authors of what he called the psychological novel (one thinks, for example, of Dostoevski) tend to distribute aspects of their personalities among the characters:

> Der psychologische Roman verdankt im ganzen wohl seine Besonderheit der Neigung des modernen Dichters, sein Ich durch Selbstbeobachtung in Partial-Ichs zu zerspalten und demzufolge die Konfliktströmungen seines Seelenlebens in mehreren Helden zu personifizieren.[1]

However, the split self does not become an immediate and necessary concern for interpretation until the underlying identity of two or more characters begins to play a role in the poetic world they inhabit. Even at this level a broad taxonomy of split or double selves confronts the reader. The phenomenon extends back in time to Plato, at least in terms of his recognition that the self contains parts which can function quasi-independently; i.e., each as a whole, and in a tripartite system much like the Freudian id, ego, and superego.[2] The split self also reaches into our midst today in the works of the American novelist Thomas McGuane. In at least two of his first three novels, *The Sporting Club* and *Ninety-Two in the Shade*, two selves are locked in conflict. One represents the seat of the author's present consciousness: socialized, reasonable, conventional; the other is an extension into adulthood of a childhood personality: tormented, self-destructive, but demonic in energy and potential. The positive advantages of both selves—or perhaps the working of the earlier self as a projection from the unconscious, locked into its relationship with the conscious—bind them inexorably together in a deadly clash.

This is the sort of split self that interests us here—two outwardly unrelated individuals caught in the paradox of requiring unity for their salvation, and at the same time knowing somehow (or acting as though with unconscious knowledge) that in such a unity one of them must be annihilated as an independent consciousness.

A more intensive contemporary development of a split self is Samuel Beckett's *Waiting for Godot* (1953). Here the two characters, "Gogo" and "Didi," wait for their synthesis and salvation in the title figure, who never appears. The initial characteristics of the two part selves are not obvious; but the crucial trend in their development is seen in the parallel master-slave figures Pozzo and Lucky. As the text makes abundantly clear, these represent a more extreme version of Gogo and Didi ten years later. If Gogo and Didi are nearly balanced in their friendship, the later relationship has deteriorated into an exhausted and sterile sadomasochism. Where the split selves examined in the present study are parts of a larger human personality, Beckett's characters function on two levels. By virtue of the structure of his name, among other things, Godot on one hand clearly suggests the yearned-for unity of two human parts. But this larger self also assumes compelling overtones of Christ. At issue here is not only a psychological human whole but also a religious whole uniting what may also be viewed as independent individuals. Without an overarching religious synthesis, Beckett seems to be saying, the axis of human love can only lose equilibrium and capsize into a suffocating hell of boredom and fatigued despair.

The existing literature on the split self has focused on something different—namely, the double as an overt replication of the main figure, or otherwise obviously related to it. In addition to a few psychological studies of largely historical interest,[3] three literary studies stand out for their attempts to come to grips with the problem.

Marianne Wain has discussed the double in the German *Romantik*, in which the second figure emerges as a reaction to the extreme solipsism of the main character. Significantly, the present undertaking, with a somewhat different perspective, passes by the *Romantik* altogether without registering anything of relevance. This suggests the breadth and variety of manifestations of the theme.[4]

Carl Keppler's study, *The Literature of the Second Self*,[5] is the most comprehensive treatment of the problem. Although in his broad approach he does not deal interpretively with individual works in detail, he does attempt a taxonomy of basic types: The Second Self as Twin Brother, Pursuer, Tempter, Vision of Horror, Saviour, Beloved, and the Second Self in Time. It is the last category that intrigues Keppler and that is most closely related to the present topic. And yet, except for a brief mention of Goethe's *Faust*, Keppler's study also does not overlap with the examples examined here.

In his psychoanalytically oriented approach: *A Psychoanalytic Study of the Double in Literature*,[6] Robert Rogers treats the question from the Freudian concept of the process of "decomposition." In this theory, the self may break apart into any number of fragments, with characteristics that are unpredictable (generally not, for example, into the tidy entities of ego, id, and superego). Rogers makes a tacit assumption that I had shared until well into this study—namely, that the fragments of self add up to one normal, whole self and that therefore we are ultimately dealing with pathology, with a personality lacking the normalcy most of us possess and take for granted. One may counter this depressing prospect only with the argument that mental illness is a kind of genius, at least in the context of poetry.

In some cases we are almost certainly dealing with such fragmentation. But in others another possibility arises which calls into question the assumption inherent in the very expression "split self" and suggests something more optimistic than the poet's struggle with the pathological. Are we sometimes dealing not with parts of one normal self, but with an attempt to integrate related whole selves? Are Götz and Weislingen each mere fragments, or do they represent whole personalities who reflect different stages in Goethe's life and who try to unite in a kind of oversoul or larger mystical unity? A temporal dimension is always implied in the topic that is presently defined. Therefore, the search for unity could be seen as an attempt to synthesize a conscious present personality with a past personality very much alive in the unconscious. This would be consistent with Jung's view of the unconscious as timeless, in which childhood experiences are as real as those from the present. In principle this distinction between part or whole self makes an enormous qualitative difference. But in critical practice is it difficult to decide and perhaps does not matter. For Götz and Weislingen are both insufficient by themselves, whole or otherwise, and both are caught in the lethal attraction that functions the same, whether or not each is viewed as less than a normal personality. Thus I have dealt with the complementarity of personalities closely tied to one another and with the definition of their individual qualities and their conflict. Left aside is the philosophical question of parts of a normal whole, or parts of a larger self integrated, in the mathematical sense, over time.

II

The present split self is quite specific in its definition. The basic pattern remains close to the following: A childhood self (usually seen outwardly as an adult) possesses the ability to love, but is oppressed by paternal influence and is juxtaposed to an adult self who possesses full emancipation from the father but lacks the ability to love. Each self thus possesses what the other needs and lacks what the other has. Both selves strive ambivalently—and only on an underlying level, not in explicit, conscious terms—for unity. They fear the annihilation that must result for one of them if unity is achieved. As a result, the conflict usually ends tragically with the failure of both selves. C.G. Jung has identified the psychological basis of the problem, or at least a major aspect of it, as it concerns us here:

> Es ist nun ein psychologischer Grundsatz, daß ein vom Bewußtsein abgespaltener Seelenteil nur anscheinend inaktiviert wird, in Wirklichkeit aber zu einer Besessenheit der Persönlichkeit führt, wodurch deren Zielsetzung im Sinne des abgespaltenen Seelenteils verfälscht wird. Wenn also der kindhafte Zustand der Kollektivseele bis zur gänzlichen Ausschließung verdrängt wird, so bemächtigt sich der unbewußte Inhalt der bewußten Zielsetzung, wodurch deren Verwirklichung gehemmt, verfälscht, oder geradezu zerstört wird. Ein lebensfähiger Fortschritt aber kommt nur zustande durch die Kooperation beider.[7]

This general principle of the continued functioning of a repressed or split-off part of the psyche takes on specific significance for us in connection with another observation:

> Das differenzierte Bewußtsein ist immer von Entwurzelung bedroht, daher es der Kompensation durch den noch vorhandenen Kindheitszustand bedarf.[8]

"Entwurzelung" corresponds closely to the present concept of emancipation. With Jung's own broad concept of libido in mind, we can safely read into this "Kompensation" the attempt to synthesize an uprooted conscious personality with a lost capability to love. The only remaining element in the present definition is the function of the father as the usual cause of the problem.

Most of the works under discussion will vary from this norm in one way or another. Götz, for example, is capable of love but not directly oppressed by the father. Lenz, Schiller, and Broch introduce a third, intermediate stage between the two others with some greater hope than they have of achieving salvation. Wedekind develops a whole scale of degrees of emancipation. But by and large the authors remain surprisingly true to the model.

Three possible reasons suggest themselves for this consistency: (1) I am forcing the pattern upon them. This possibility arises particularly where I disagree with another writer who has seen the split self differently. Still, despite my efforts to stand back from the pattern and look at the texts with a neutral eye, the basic constellation kept reasserting itself. In one sense, however, the consistency of theme is in fact artificial. It must be acknowledged that there may be other ways of defining the same phenomenon. The process of socialization, for example, would serve to distinguish between the unique and gifted child and the more conventional, stale or tired personality of the adult. But the question of socialization, by itself, does not apply as widely or as specifically as the essentially Jungian pattern I have used. (2) The poets simply copied one another, repeating the theme as they saw it in a predecessor. To a significant extent such influences did help to propagate and stabilize the theme, as we shall see. Each author was quite ready and able, however, to vary and develop it to suit his own concerns. (3) The theme contains archetypal substance. Since most of the authors were reflecting—in a stylized way—their own conflicts in their development of the theme, this possibility, in conjunction with the use of earlier sources, would seem to account adequately for the continuity of the theme, particularly in view of Jung's comments quoted above.

Other levels of textual explanation besides this psychological principle also enter and parallel the relationship between oppressed child and emancipated adult. These begin with Goethe's Herderian concern for the passing from a heroic medieval world to a weak (socialized?) modern society. Schiller emphasizes the moral dimension of the polarity between the two selves, and Lenz introduces a criticism of the nobility. Wedekind mounts an attack against bourgeois values, and Broch reflects in his split selves the "Disintegration of Values" in European history. But these levels do not supplant the personal and psychological; rather, they run parallel to it and by themselves cannot account for the texts.

Notes

1. "The psychological novel owes its peculiarity in general to the tendency of the modern poet to split his ego in self-examination into partial egos and consequently to personify the conflicts of his psychic life in several heroes." (Sigmund Freud, "Der Dichter und das Phantasieren," in *Gesammelte Werke*, vol. 7, ed. Anna Freud et al. [Frankfurt a/M: S. Fischer, 1941], pp. 220–21.)

2. Cf. Robert Rogers, *A Psychoanalytic Study of the Double in Literature* (Detroit, Mich.; Wayne State University Press, 1970), pp. 9–10.

3. Cf. Carl Keppler's discussion of the literature in Chap. 9 of his *The Literature of the Second Self* (Tucson: University of Arizona Press, 1972).

4. Marianne Wain, "The Double in Romantic Narrative: A Preliminary Study," *Germanic Review* 36 (4) (December, 1961): 258–68.

5. Op. cit.

6. Op. cit.

7. "It is a basic psychological principle that a part of the psyche split off from consciousness only appears to be inactivated, but in reality leads to an obsession of the personality, whereby the latter's goal-setting behavior is falsified in the sense of the split-off part. Thus when the childlike condition of the collective soul is repressed to the point of total exclusion, the unconscious content assumes control over this conscious goal-setting, whereby the realization of the latter is inhibited, falsified or even destroyed. Healthy progress only comes into being through the cooperation of both." (C. G. Jung and Karl Kerényi, *Das göttliche Kind*, "Albae Vigiliae," 6/7 [N.p.: Pantheon Akademische Verlagsanstalt, 1940], p. 102).

8. "The differentiated consciousness is always threatened by uprooting; thus it requires compensation by the still present childhood condition." (Ibid., p. 101).

The Split Self
from Goethe to Broch

Part I

The authors to be discussed center on the Storm and Stress and Expressionism—two related periods characterized by youthfulness and rebellion against social, frequently paternal norms. Only Grillparzer and Broch lie outside these movements, and Broch may be viewed in the use of this theme as having carried over Kafka's Expressionism. The same reduction, however, cannot be made in the case of Grillparzer. Therefore, I decided against labeling parts 1 and 2 "Storm and Stress" and "Expressionism."

Still, the emergence of the split-self theme in the Storm and Stress movement is no accident, but, with its concern ultimately with the self of the poet, manifests one of the innermost intellectual currents of the time. H.A. Korff, in his classic *Geist der Goethezeit*, grasped and defined this new spirit:

> Wer in der Kunst Genuß sucht, erfasst das Kunstwerk mit den Kategorien der eigenen Individualität. Wer aber das Kunstwerk als eine Offenbarung versteht, der gibt mit dieser Hingabe an die Eigenart des Künstlers seine Eigenart auf. Sein kleines Ich versinkt in einem größeren. Das ist die neue Würde der Kunst unter dem Gesichtspunkte der symbolischen Kunstauffassung.[1]

The world outside the self is also expressed in the work, but only after it is transformed and made part of the self:

> Daß der Dichter nicht nur seine Persönlichkeit, sondern in seiner Persönlichkeit das ganze Erdreich, in dem sie wurzelte, mit zum Ausdruck brachte, gerade das gab dem von ihm geschaffenen Kunstwerke jene Tiefe, von der der Rationalismus, der darin nur den Ausdruck bewußten Planens sah, gar keine Ahnung hatte.[2]

The projection of the poet's most intimate concerns into a medium to be shared by the public suggests his attempt to commune with his readers, present and future, as they realize and recreate in their own consciousness the experience the poet set down. Indeed, each reader actually creates a new work, in a limited sense, joining to the poet's world his own emotions, experiences, and preconceptions. This is communion of poet and public in its deepest sense. Goethe hinted at something like this in a comment on *Götz:*

> Als ich meinen "Götz" herausgab, war das eine meiner angenehmsten Hoffnungen, meine Freunde, deren ich doch manche in der weiten Welt habe, würden sich nach mir umsehen, und angenehmer sich mein erinnern, als wenn ich eine lange unbedeutende Verbindung mit ihnen unterhalten hätte.[3]

Like the other poets of the split self, who exposed themselves so totally in their works, Goethe disguised the relationship between the two central personalities. Perhaps this reflects a feeling that "the" public is a bit unselective and promiscuous for such a sharing of self. When Goethe referred to his friends, he must have been aware that he was communicating with those who would respond to the work on the same personal level that he projected into it. This group would be far smaller than the public as a whole, for most of them were absorbed by the outermost layer of knightly heroism.

Notes

1. "He who seeks pleasure in art grasps the work of art with the categories of his own individuality. But he who understands the work of art as a revelation yields his individuality to that of the artist. His little ego sinks into a larger one. That is the new dignity of art from the point of view of the symbolic concept of art." (H. A. Korff, *Geist der Goethezeit*, 3 vols., [Leipzig: J. J. Weber, 1923], 1: 128–29).

2. "That the poet brought to expression not only his personality, but in his personality the entire world in which it was rooted—precisely that gave the work of art he created that depth of which rationalism—which saw only the expression of conscious planning—had no inkling whatsoever." (Ibid., pp. 130–31).

3. "When I published my 'Götz' it was one of my most pleasant hopes that my friends, of whom I have many in the world, would take notice of me and remember me more positively than if I had maintained a long, insignificant connection with them." (Letter to E. T. Langer, Oct. 27, 1973. From H. A. Gräf, *Goethe über seine Dichtungen* [Frankfurt a/M: Rütter und Loening, 1906], Drama III, p. 37).

1

Goetz von Berlichingen and the Young Goethe

I

THE present-day reception of Goethe's *Götz von Berlichingen* (1773), according to Fritz Martini, is largely consistent, both in Germany and elsewhere, in its rejection of the play as no longer relevant today:

> Ronald Peacocks Urteil: *"Götz von Berlichingen* has always seemed to me . . . rather a tedious play for non-Germans" ist weitgehend auch ein Urteil der deutschen Leser geworden. . . . "The real trouble is that we do not feel involved at all in the life of the play. Finally, if we are to be moved by a work, we have to be able to identify ourselves with some of the characters in some of their situations, we have to see them involved humanly, in problems related to our own, or potentially so."[1]

Peacock suggests, reasonably, that a work of literature should contain a significance not solely restricted to its time; presumably, then, it should deal with some sort of universal social or psychological problem beneath the level of its external particulars. But one recent interpretation of the play suggests precisely that: a basis for our human identification with this creation of the eighteenth century; i.e., a psychological level of significance just as valid today as in Goethe's time.

In her essay on the two versions of the play, Ilse A. Graham

has identified Weislingen as Götz's "alter ego" and has placed
the problem of two parts of one self at the focal point of the
text:

> Denn aus formalen Beziehungen in allen Teilen des
> Dramas geht es hervor, daß Weislingen—eine vom Dichter
> frei erfundene Figur—als Teil der Person des Helden zu
> verstehen ist. Er ist Götzens rechte Hand. All das, wonach
> Weislingen greift und was er genießt, bestimmt für uns
> erstmalig den Bereich, aus dem Götz seines Gebrechens
> wegen ausgeschlossen bleibt: die mondäne Erotik am bi-
> schöflichen Hof und, genauer gesagt: Adelheid. In dem
> zentralen Symbol des Dramas—der Hand, die nicht berüh-
> ren darf—ist ein so strenges Tabu ausgedrückt, daß diese
> weltliche Sphäre völlig abgetrennt bleibt von der eigentli-
> chen Mitte der Handlung, in der Götz dominiert.
> Demgemäß erweist sich der zentrifugale Bau des Dramas als
> unablässig bedingt von der zentrifugalen Sprengkraft des
> Hauptsymbols, dem ein gewaltiger Gefühlswert inne-
> wohnt.[2]

Martini devotes much of the first part of his essay to the
rejection of *Götz* as historically and sociologically irrelevant
and inconsequential, then dismisses Graham's psychological
interpretation as emphasizing the work too much as a character drama (p.39). He would apparently prefer to require a
sociological interpretation, whether it works or not. The difficulty is due both to Graham's arguable devaluation of
Weislingen to an appendage of Götz (to be discussed below)
and to Martini's apparent assumption that the play must
achieve its coherence entirely on one level, rather than simultaneously in a public, historical dimension and in a more
private, psychological symbolism.

If Graham's view is essentially correct, then it radically
revises the traditional view of Goethe's first major work. It has
been regarded as a brilliant but erratic and somewhat imma-
ture application of a Shakespeare superficially perceived in
terms of disregard for the dramatic unities. It has also been
likened to a Herder rather spongily absorbed with his call for
folksongs, his idealizing of the Middle Ages, his Rousseauean

contempt for modern civilization, and his attention to the cultural evolution of language. Certainly, Goethe transformed all these ideas into his own immediate esthetic self-directives. Still, the play has seemed traditionally to be as much a realization of Herder's theories as an original achievement of Goethe.[3]

But Graham's interpretation subordinates the play's externals to an original and subtle Goethean psychology. As we proceed to develop this point of view, it is crucial that we first evaluate the evidence for the symbolism of two part-selves, as opposed to the mere complementarity of two friends. The evidence begins with the ideas Herder expounded to his youthful disciple in 1770 and 1771. One of these, in all probability, was the comparison of the ages of a culture to the developmental stages of the individual (published 1774 in *Auch eine Philosophie der Geschichte zur Bildung der Menschheit*). This idea accompanied the view that the era of knightly individualism was replaced by a weak, modern society, such as the one rejected by Rousseau.

The play indeed depicts the gap between an idealized, medieval knighthood of Götz and the modern collectivism of Weislingen. If the two are in fact parts of one self representing different temporal stages, then it would become highly probable that Goethe had taken Herder's comparison of individual and societal development to heart; that what appears to be a Herderian comment on history is also a statement about a parallel development in an individual from a heroic past (childhood) to a self-betraying accommodation to society. This interpretation follows easily, if such a split self can be justified in the text.

Since Graham has discussed individual motifs in some detail, it will suffice here to focus on a few main questions. To begin with, the entire tragic course of the play is generated by the failure of Götz and Weislingen to unite in some sense. The peculiarly weak external necessity for Götz's failure and demise can be designated as irrelevant.[4] Two factors determine Weislingen's flight from Götz: the sexual attraction of Adelheid and the fear of domination by his childhood friend. The latter theme includes explicit references to the split self:

In Berlichingens Gewalt! von dem ich mich kaum losgear-
beitet habe, dessen Andenken ich mied wie Feuer, den ich
hoffte zu überwältigen! Und er—der alte treuherzige Götz!
Heiliger Gott, was will, will aus dem allen werden? Rück-
geführt, Adelbert, in den Saal! wo wir als Buben unsere
Jagd trieben—da du ihn liebtest, an ihm hingst wie an
deiner Seele. Wer kann ihm nahen und ihn hassen? Ach!
ich bin so ganz nichts hier! Glückselige Zeiten, ihr seid
vorbei.[5]

If taken literally, the references to Götz as Weislingen's
"soul" and to his being "nothing" in Götz's domain directly
suggest the problem of the split self. The latter reference, in
particular, focuses on the fundamental problem of two part-
selves who have become separate physical individuals. They
must lock in deadly conflict, for if either self gains the positive
aspect of personality possessed by the other, that other half
becomes superfluous and is destroyed. In any union of Götz
and Weislingen the latter would cease to exist as an independent entity. The tragic paradox for Weislingen is that to yield
to Götz would mean to sacrifice his identity, while to remain
separate is to remain incomplete. Thus Weislingen is correct
in sensing the threat from Götz, is indeed "imprisoned" by
him in more than an external sense. But Götz refuses to force
the issue: "Wenn Euer Gewissen rein ist, so seid Ihr frei
(p.91)".[6] This is not merely a polite appeal to Weislingen's
sense of honor, but a statement of psychological fact. In
emancipating himself from the knightly world of their childhood, Weislingen has paid for his apparent freedom with a
guilty conscience associated with the betrayal of his values.
Liebetraut's words apply to him:

Ich wollte lieber das Geheul der Totenglocke und ominös-
er Vögel, . . . als von Laufern, Springern und andern
Bestien das ewige: "Schach dem König!" *Bischof.* Wem
wird auch das einfallen! *Liebetraut.* Einem zum Exempel,
der schwach wäre und ein stark Gewissen hätte, wie denn
das meistenteils beisammen ist. (P. 105)[7]

Yet for all his weakness and guilty conscience, Weislingen
enjoys one major advantage which Götz had not anticipated,

and which saves him at the last minute from some sort of oblivion of ego: Adelheid, and the principle of love or sexuality she represents.

The question of Weislingen's advantage over Götz is crucial and problematic, and must be dealt with in the context of Götz's part-nature. That he represents, first of all, not only a past age, but also childhood, is suggested by the nostalgic memories of the old days, when the two friends played together amidst the colorful life and pageantry of the castle, and when Götz dominated. Now Götz's castle seems deserted and lonely, while the center of social life has moved to the bishop's court. The uncertainty arises with the interpretation of Götz's missing hand, the leitmotiv of the play. Graham's concept of the missing hand as a symbol of missing vitality[8] depends on one passage in particular: "Meine Rechte, obgleich im Kriege nicht unbrauchbar, ist gegen den Druck der Liebe unempfindlich (p.81)."[9] As Götz's missing hand, Weislingen displays—despite his vitality—a marked weakness of character that results from his being not a person at all, but only a principle, an appendage.

While Graham's idea of a taboo, symbolized by the iron hand, is tempting, the specific suggestion here of Götz's inability to love is not confirmed by the rest of the play. This reading of "gegen den Druck der Liebe unempfindlich" might also be explained as an inevitable, external aspect of the iron hand not intended in itself to define Götz's character. Other references to the motif suggest an alternative. One passage specifies, to begin with, a more co-equal status of Weislingen than results from Graham's reading:

Ach! nun ist mein Traum aus. Mir war's heute nacht, ich gäb dir meine rechte eiserne Hand, und du hieltest mich so fest, daß sie aus den Armschienen ging wie abgebrochen. (Pp. 99–100)[10]

Weislingen need not be equated directly with the missing hand, despite one suggestion of this: "Ich hoffte, Adalbert wird künftig meine rechte Hand sein" (p.90).[11] It would seem more reasonable to see him as *possessing* the attribute missing from Götz. Götz's character and situation suggest that this is not the ability to love, but rather love itself. Götz is betrayed and deserted by his alter ego and by the new age he represents. Thus the problem of love is superimposed upon and totally integrated with the fact of the split self. Love appears as the expression not so much of vitality as of human unity. This interpretation of the play's central theme is confirmed by the otherwise irrelevant scene where the two farmers, having drained their resources in litigation, solve their dispute through the marriage of their children. In this way, they gladly give them the land they could not wrest from one another and thus transcend their division through love and unification.

This view of Götz's problem; i.e., his deprivation and betrayal, is also commensurate with the contrastingly negative sense in which Weislingen possesses love. His relationship to Adelheid and his betrayal of Marie make clear that what he possesses is not vitality in any inner, larger sense, but a strictly negative erotic sexuality (a problem that also concerned Goethe in *Faust*). In the first version of 1771 Marie's description of her lessons in the convent defines Weislingen's kind of love:

> Meine Abtissin verglich die Lieb auch offt den Blüten. Weh dem rief sie offt der sie bricht! Er hat den Saamen von Tausend Glückseligkeiten zerstöret. Einen Augenblick Genuß, und sie welckt hinweg und wird hingeworfen in einen verachteten Winckel zu verdorren und zu verfaulen.[12]

Thus, Weislingen's advantage of erotic sexuality is bought at the expense of a more intrinsic unity and integrity, and is punished by the unfaithfulness of a cynical seductress. Weislingen becomes a melancholy "sick poet" (p.117), and his relationship with Adelheid soon exposes his inner impotence. Götz, conversely, is inwardly whole, but externally incomplete as a result of Weislingen's betrayal of their unity. As the heroic childhood self he is doomed to obsolescence and loneliness. The world simply no longer provides him with the appropriate Arthurian original for Weislingen's distasteful courtly milieu.

If a degree of confusion still hovers around this interpretation, it is due to the fact that the love which is the central issue here is not, in fact, solely a matter of the unity of two individuals, but also—and this is a characteristically Goethean dimension—of the admiration afforded the individual by the social milieu. While Weislingen possesses the latter, Götz is externally deprived of this social attention. In developmental terms, Weislingen (the real, as opposed to the ideal, seat of Goethe's identification) has sacrificed an inner capability in order to bask in the superficial, illusory love afforded by the bishop's court. What Götz lacks and legitimately needs, then—a loving social milieu—appears in Weislingen as something false, a betrayal of self. Götz requires the lost knightly world of his childhood, while Weislingen panders his soul to a corrupt present.

This pattern does not entirely conform to our hypothesis. With his emancipation from the childhood milieu and his intrinsic loss of the ability to love, Weislingen corresponds to the uprooted adult personality we defined in our Introduction. Götz, as childhood self, possesses the ability to love (here seen more in terms of inner integrity) but does not suffer from the balancing disadvantage of paternal oppression. Instead, his disadvantage consists in an external deprivation imposed by Weislingen as the embodiment of a new social order. The missing element of paternal oppression, while not directly a problem for Götz, nevertheless asserts itself indirectly elsewhere in the text as a more immediate concern of Goethe as the unifying identity behind his characters.

II

In order to obtain a better idea of what this highly personal material meant to its author and to gain a clearer insight into the text, we must turn to Goethe's autobiography. While a complete understanding of the real Goethe would be impossible, we are concerned here not with the totality of his experience and unconscious mental life, but with an abstracted, partly fictionalized self in his own consciousness. (Of course the unconscious Goethe may very well manifest himself in his works, but not primarily on the level of manipulated formal structure that concerns us in the analysis of the split self.)

As noted in the Introduction, the split self, as narrowly defined for the present context, entails a sudden shift between some variation of a childhood stage of paternally oppressed genius or ability to love, and an adult personality of emancipation coupled with the inability to love.

Frank Ryder has noted in Götz's present situation a contradiction between his declared insistence on total freedom and his avowal of obedience to the emperor.[13] Such a conflict does exist, at least logically, and would seem to parallel a psychological conflict between obedience to the father and the need for emancipation. Not only a father conflict, but the crucial sudden shift in milieu occurred in Goethe's life.

Goethe's description of his childhood in *Dichtung und Wahrheit* reveals that he enjoyed a great deal of love and admiration showered on him by family and relatives, including his father, who, despite any conflicts, largely devoted himself to the education of his talented son. But this very pedagogical devotion of an otherwise largely idle father placed a heavy burden on the boy. Thus, when the time approached to depart for Leipzig, the eighteen-year-old felt as though he were breaking out of a prison:

> Die heimliche Freude eines Gefangenen, wenn er seine Ketten abgelöst und die Kerkergitter bald durchgefeilt hat, kann nicht größer sein, als die meine war, indem ich die Tage schwinden und den Oktober herannahen sah. . . . genug, ich sah nur meine gegenwärtigen Verhältnisse düster, und stellte mir die übrige unbekannte Welt licht und heiter vor.[14]

Both the feeling of oppression and a kind of Golden Age of childhood—an ambivalent mixture, to be sure—were suddenly left behind when he went to Leipzig. Here he found himself in a totally different environment. Whereas virtually the entire city of Frankfurt, it seemed, had belonged psychologically to his family milieu (his grandfather had been *Schultheiss* and the young Wolfgang was granted, for example, privileged access to various public buildings), in Leipzig his expectations of finding everything "bright and cheerful" were rudely disappointed. Indeed, his childhood world suddenly disappeared forever. No one knew or cared much about him. His clothes, made in the house at his father's direction, were ridiculous and had to be sold—probably with a painful feeling of betrayal of his father's values and taste. His dialect was also subjected to ridicule, specifically due to the use of crude expressions (cf. the language of Götz), and all this had to be overcome.

In the shock of this sudden uprooting and threat to his personality, Goethe reached out for support. He had to make Leipzig society love him the way his family and seemingly Frankfurt had loved him. This new adjustment entailed the denial of his earlier childhood individuality in favor of a more urbane socialization (cf. his feeling of being controlled by society [*Dichtung und Wahrheit*, pp. 254,306,346], as well as the character of Weislingen). He had to acquire new clothes, learn social graces, and play the hated games of polite society (cf. Liebetraut's hatred of chess). Since such measures obviously had to fail to recreate his childhood milieu, he complemented them with the attachment to an older friend, specifically one who was emancipated and socially self-sufficient. In Leipzig this was Behrisch, who delighted him with his clownish individualism and social aggressiveness, when, for example, he indulged in analyzing and denigrating the dress and gait of passersby. In Strassburg this role was played by Herder, in an intellectual context, and then by Merck, who as a practical businessman was a convenient supplement to Herder. All three shared the more or less cynical emancipation *a la* Mephisto that Goethe needed to protect himself in a world that had suddenly ceased to give him the love and recognition of his childhood.

When Goethe returned from Leipzig to Frankfurt it was as a "castaway" (p.337), as one who had barely managed to survive the shock of the larger society. He had barely thrown up defenses, including a marked tendency to melancholy (cf. Weislingen here also), and had as yet no clear idea of how to regain his childhood identity, which was now inaccessible for purely temporal reasons. After his experience in Leipzig, his stay in Strassburg then added a second vaccination against the shock of adjusting to society. Here Goethe was able to apply the lessons of Leipzig and to mature from his tyrannical ego and childish tantrums with Annette Schönkopf to a more gentle and lyric relationship with Friederike Brion. Here also enters the new element of guilt feelings for the inability (or at least failure) to love.

Goethe's infatuation with this young village girl, untainted by social affectations, was drawn out by the fact that he had to shuttle back and forth between Sesenheim and Strassburg in order to see her. By the time he had begun to tire of her— since no deeper bond had established itself on his part— infatuation was replaced not by the boredom of an imprisoning relationship, but by a feeling of guilt that arose from the knowledge that he would soon be leaving her, simply because his studies in Strassburg would be completed. To prolong their relationship would force him into making an unwanted commitment, perhaps marriage. Thus we find a basic pattern: his ambivalent childhood of love and (as he saw it) oppression; his sudden, traumatic shift to an indifferent social milieu; and his resulting state of emancipation from his father (partly for the superficial but important reason of geography), coupled with the inability or failure to love. In Goethe's case the latter condition seems to have been compounded by a feeling of insecurity about his capabilities and his future as an artist. Herder did not help matters. He specifically denigrated Goethe's childhood, for example, when the latter was incautious enough to yearn for it aloud in his presence (p.403). It was only after the publication of *Götz* that Goethe began to win from society some of the attention that had been left behind in childhood.

Goethe does not directly mention a split self. But he does afford us a biographical clue to this problem. In the beginning of *Dichtung und Wahrheit* he retells at length the story of Genesis, then justifies this by explaining that this material was a center around which the many other influences upon him organized themselves (pp. 140–141). While no split self can be found in Genesis, the underlying problem of alienation and emancipation from the father is reflected in Joseph, who was driven from home and subsequently became great and powerful.

Goethe made no attempt to conceal his childhood delusions of grandeur; for example, when the hero of his "Märchen" asserts his affinity to the gods, thus overwhelming his opponent in the figure of the park overseer (a father figure?). This can be compared to the fairy tale told by Götz's son Karl in which a child cures "King and Emperor." Heinrich Meyer notes that as a child Goethe painted himself as Joseph in pictures that were later found at the home of Count Thoranc.[15] Thus we can appreciate the shock Goethe experienced when he read Book Two of Moses:

> Man weiß, wie ich schon früher mich in den Zustand der Urwelt, die uns das erste Buch Mosis schildert, einzuweihen suchte. Weil ich nun schrittweise und ordentlich zu verfahren dachte, so griff ich, nach einer langen Unterbrechung, das zweite Buch an. Allein welch ein Unterschied! Gerade wie die kindliche Fülle aus meinem Leben verschwunden war, so fand ich auch das zweite Buch von dem ersten durch eine ungeheure Kluft getrennt. Das völlige Vergessen vergangener Zeit spricht sich schon aus in den wenigen bedeutenden Worten: "Da kam ein neuer König auf in Aegypten, der wußte nichts von Joseph."[16]

Goethe makes no attempt here to disguise his identification with Joseph, who served as an archetype for his own image of an earlier self in a lost childhood paradise. The parallel to *Götz* is also clear, in the light of Herder's comparison of Biblical antiquity with the childhood of civilization. The chief difference is that in *Götz* the lost childhood is placed in the Middle Ages, as a time contiguous with the emergence of the weak modern collectivism to which Goethe had yielded in Leipzig.

III

Returning to the text of *Götz*, quasi over the shoulder of Goethe (we hope!), we can see the significance of some further details of the play that might otherwise appear anomalous. Above all, the emotional overtones of the play become more distinct in an autobiographical context. The key to this secondary, more personal level is Götz's son Karl, a clear reflection by Goethe on his own childhood. Like the young Wolfgang, Karl is encouraged to retell a fairy tale, and here specifically one that emphasizes a child's hand as a source of healing, with obvious relevance to Götz's infirmity. The ability of the child to cure "King and Emperor" suggests a reconciliation of son and father through the dominance of the son—presumably the one way Goethe could have retained his childhood environment in a manner satisfactory to him. Thus, after returning from Leipzig he criticized his father's taste in interior decoration, knowing it would hurt his feelings, but perhaps hoping he would accept his son's independence and esthetic authority (*Dichtung und Wahrheit*, pp. 424–25).

In any case, Karl's powers exist only vicariously in his story, while his weakness is palpable, including his inability, significantly, to connect (to accept?) his own father with his name and title. That Karl and Götz both represent, on one level or another, Goethe's childhood self (Karl more the real, Götz the ideal) is suggested in a passage from the first version in which Götz compares himself to the emperor: "Ich lieb ihn, denn wir haben einerley Schicksal." He then lists the emperor's frustrations:

Ich weiß, er wünscht sich manchmal lieber Todt, als länger die Seele eines so krüplichen Körpers zu seyn. Ruft er zum Fuse Marsch, der ist eingeschlafen, zum Arm heb dich, der ist verrenckt, und wenn ein Gott im Gehirn säs, er könnt nicht mehr tuhn als ein unmü[n]dig Kind, die Speculationen und Wünsche ausgenommen, um die er nur noch schlimmer dran ist.[17]

The "dependent child" is reflected in Karl; the "god in his brain" is a projection of Goethe's self ideal (partly embodied in Götz); and the reference to "Speculations . . ." reflects the awareness that such an ideal, like Karl's fairy tale, is far from reality.

Thus Goethe plays subtly—perhaps gingerly—with the father-son relationship. This is not directly or obviously inherent in Götz, who does not himself reflect childhood oppression as the earlier self. Goethe uses Götz both as an ideal self and as a father figure, the failure to follow whose example damns the son. The contrast to Karl is the resourceful gypsy boy who knows all the brooks and paths, as Götz had as a child, and who, like Karl, also holds an apple—a Biblical reference to the sin of failing to follow the directions of the father. The emperor, as father figure in Karl's fairy tale, serves as a bridge to the real Kaiser, who is a father figure for Götz and whose son is also named Karl and resembles Weislingen. That Adelheid has plans to ingratiate herself with this latter Karl completes a finely drawn circle of relationships.

A remaining question of import is where Goethe, standing at the beginning of what amounts almost to a traditional theme in German literature, himself derived it. We have discussed his identification with Joseph and his sudden loss of childhood, paralleled in Götz and Weislingen and by Herder's theory of history. This background is perhaps sufficient to account for the genesis of the theme as a psychological problem. An additional possibility suggests itself as a source for the use of the theme specifically as a literary device. In his admiration for and imitation of Shakespeare, Goethe emphasized in his Shakespeare essay of 1773 the expression of the English poet's self in his work:

> Seine Stücke drehen sich alle um den geheimen Punkt, den noch kein Philosoph gesehen und bestimmt hat, in dem das Eigentümliche unsres Ich, die prätendierte Freiheit unsres Wollens, mit dem notwendigen Gang des Ganzen zusammenstößt.[18]

In view of his attempt to imitate Shakespeare in *Götz* it is not unreasonable to consider whether his procedure in this play was intended to realize this same Shakespearean characteristic. But it is difficult to say exactly what he meant by "the peculiarity of our self" clashing with plot or fate. Certainly, the superficial sense of this constitutes no "secret point." The obvious place to look for elaboration is Herder, under whose theoretical dominance Goethe still stood at the time of his essay, particularly in regard to Shakespeare.

In his own Shakespeare essay Herder keeps repeating his central point of a unifying "whole" in the works of the Bard. For the most part he neglects to specify exactly what he means by this, but one passage affords a crucial insight:

> . . . so sieht man, die ganze Welt ist zu diesem großen Geiste [of Shakespeare] allein Körper: alle Auftritte der Natur an diesem Körper Glieder, wie *alle Charaktere* und Denkarten *zu diesem Geiste Züge* [italics mine]—und das Ganze mag jener Riesengott des Spinoza "Pan! Universum!" heißen.[19]

He also refers to "every whole, healthy person" (p.577) suggesting a concept of healthy psychic integration in agreement with Goethe's development of the split self. Within the larger context of the work as the Creation of its author, Herder is referring directly to the split self. If this can be taken together with Goethe's references to a "secret point," "the peculiarity of our self," and a "whole" in Shakespeare, then we have here in fact a direct theoretical confirmation of the split self as well as a literary model. Shakespeare, then, appears as the likely ultimate source for this theme, first recognized by Herder, then transformed by Goethe and reborn in *Götz* specifically as a problem of dual selves.

IV

After *Götz*, Goethe continued to make use of the theme of the split self, with shifting accents. In *Faust* the archetypal emancipated self, incapable of love, is Mephisto. Faust is not, however, a complementary half, but a fundamentally whole self, including the flaw manifested so blatantly by his companion. It is Faust himself who, unable to love Gretchen, indulges in the *Walpurgisnacht* while she destroys herself. Here we meet no carry-over of a childhood ideal, but rather an essentially whole adult with a crucial failing and no potential source of salvation.

At a somewhat greater distance to *Götz* is *Werther*, where Goethe much later, in "An Werther," implied two selves: "zum Bleiben ich, zum Scheiden du erkoren,/Gingst du voran—und hast nicht viel verloren."[20] Werther, as a passionate and—underneath this—egotistical self, is destroyed in favor of the "editor." The latter, as the poet Goethe, disengages himself from the doomed Werther-self as though from a chrysalis. This identity of two selves is subtly implied by the fact that the editor relates the intimate and unwritten thoughts of his subject, beyond what is contained in the letters—a surface inconsistency Goethe could easily have avoided had he wished to do so.

A further example of the split self, in the broad sense, is found in *Iphigenia*, where Thoas, as the Weimar Goethe, must renounce his hold on Iphigenia (as a reflection of Charlotte von Stein) in favor of a more youthful, pre-Weimar version of himself in Orestes (from whose perspective Iphigenia presumably reflects Goethe's sister Cornelia). The renunciation of Iphigenia in favor of an earlier self conveys a good deal of sublimation and above all a bitter irony. It might be appropriate to consider Goethe's motto to a section of *Dichtung und Wahrheit*: "Was man in der Jugend wünscht, hat man im Alter die Fülle." (P. 217)[21]

Notes

1. "Ronald Peacock's judgment, '*Götz von Berlichingen* has always seemed to me . . . rather a tedious play for non-Germans' has to a large extent also become the judgment of the German readers . . . ." (Fritz Martini, "Goethes *Götz von Berlichingen:* Charakterdrama und Gesellschaftsdrama," in *Dichten und Lesen*, ed. Ferdinand van Ingen et al. [Utrechese Publikaties voor algemene Literatuurwetenschap; Groningen: Wolters-Noordhoff, 1972], 28 – 46, p. 28).

2. "For formal relationships in all parts of the drama point to the fact that Weislingen—a figure invented by the poet—is to be understood as part of the person of the hero. He is Götz's right hand. Everything for which he reaches and which he enjoys determines for the first time the area from which Götz remains excluded as a result of his weakness: the worldly eroticism at the bishop's court and, more specifically: Adelheid. In the central symbol of the drama—the hand which is not permitted to touch—is expressed a taboo so strict that this worldly sphere remains completely separated from the actual center of the plot, in which Götz dominates. Thus the centrifugal structure of the drama demonstrates itself as continually determined by the centrifugal explosiveness of the main symbol, in which a powerful emotional value resides." (Ilse A. Graham, "Vom *Urgötz* zum *Götz:* Neufassung oder Neuschöpfung?" *Jahrbuch der deutschen Schillergesellschaft* 9 [1965]: 245 – 82, 249).

3. Placed in Reformation Germany, the play presents Götz as a rather lonely but steadfast knight trying to preserve his independence and help the oppressed. His

opponent is the Bishop of Bamberg, representing the new, collectivist society controlled by the "Nichtswürdigen." The decisive figure in the struggle is Götz's childhood friend Weislingen, torn between loyalty to Götz and his social ambitions. Captured by Götz, Weislingen decides to stay with him and marry his sister Marie, but he is lured away by the arrival of the seductive Adelheid at the Bishop's court. After some successful battles against the forces of the bishop and the duped Emperor, Götz allies himself with the Farmers' Revolt. He is captured and ends up dying and broken. Weislingen, having married the treacherous Adelheid, is finally poisoned by her, and she is delivered to a secret tribunal for punishment.

4. In her more recent volume, *Goethe and Lessing: The Wellsprings of Creation* (London: Elek Books, 1973), Graham argues (p.46) that the dramatic disunity of the play—particularly that of time—directly symbolizes a disunity within Götz (as manifested outwardly in his rift with Weislingen).

5. "In Berlichingen's power! from whom I have hardly worked myself free, the thought of whom I avoided like fire, whom I hoped to overcome! And he—the old true-hearted Götz! Lord in Heaven, what is all this leading to? Returned, Adalbert, to the room!—where we chased around as children—when you loved him, clung to him as to your soul. Who can approach him and hate him? O, I am nothing here! Happy times, you are gone" *(Goethes Werke*, vol. 4 [Hamburger Ausgabe] [Hamburg: Christian Wegner Verlag, 1953], p.89). All quotations from Goethe's works are taken from this edition, with the exception of the 1771 version of *Götz (Die Geschichte Gottfriedens von Berlichingen)*.

6. "If your conscience is clear, you are free."

7. "I would rather [hear] the tolling of the death bell and ominous birds . . . than from rooks, knights, and other beasts that eternal 'Check!' *Bishop.* Who would think of that! *Liebetraut.* Someone, for example, who was weak and had a strong conscience, as these usually go together."

8. "Vom *Urgötz* zum *Götz*," p.248.

9. "My right hand, although not unusable in war, is insensitive to the touch of love."

10. "O, now my dream is gone! It seemed to me last night that I was giving you my right, iron hand, and you held me so tightly that it came out of the arm brace as though it were broken off."

11. "I hoped Adalbert would be my right hand in the future."

12. "My superior often also compared love to flowers. Let him beware, she often exclaimed, who breaks it! He has destroyed the seed of a thousand joys. A moment of pleasure and it wilts away to be thrown into a neglected corner to desiccate and rot." (J. W. von Goethe, *Goethe: Götz von Berlichingen*, ed. Jutta Neuendorff-Fürstenau [Berlin: Akademie Verlag, 1958], p.65).

13. Frank G. Ryder, "Toward a Revaluation of Goethe's Götz: The Protagonist," *PMLA* 77 (1962); 58–70.

14. "The secret joy of a prisoner, when he has loosened his chains and filed through the bars, can not be greater than mine was when I saw the days disappear and October approach. . . . enough, I saw only my present circumstances as bleak and imagined the unknown outside world to be bright and cheerful." *(Goethes Werke*, vol. 9 [Hamburger Ausgabe], p.242).

15. Heinrich Meyer, *Goethe: Das Leben im Werk* (Hamburg-Bergedorf: Stromverlag, 1949), p.53.

16. "It is known how I tried to initiate myself into the condition of the ancient world as described in Book One of Moses. Because I intended to proceed step-by-step in an orderly way I attacked, after a long interruption, the second book. But what a difference! Just as the childlike richness had disappeared from my life, I

found the second book separated from the first by an abyss. The complete disappearance of past times is already expressed in a few significant words: 'Now there arose a new king over Egypt, who did not know Joseph' ": *(Dichtung und Wahrheit, op. cit.*, p.511).

17. "I love him, for we share the same fate. . . . I know, he would sometimes rather be dead than remain the soul of such a crippled body. If he calls 'March!' to his foot, it has fallen asleep, 'Rise!' to his arm, it is out of joint, and if a god were seated in his brain he could not do more than a dependent child—aside from all the speculations and wishes, which only make things worse." (Neuendorff-Fürstenau, *op.cit.*, pp.172–73).

18. "His plays all revolve around the secret point which no philosopher has yet seen and formulated, in which the uniqueness of our self, the supposed freedom of our will clashes with the necessary course of the whole" ("Zum Shakespeares Tag," *Goethes Werke*, vol. 12, p.226).

19. "So we see, the whole world is the body for this great mind [of Shakespeare]: all scenes of nature members of this body, and *all characters* and ways of thinking *aspects of this mind* [italics mine]—and the whole may be called that giant Lord of Spinoza: 'Pan! Universum!' " (Johann Gottfried Herder, "Shakespeare," in *Sturm und Drang: Kritische Schriften* [Heidelberg: Verlag Lambert Schneider, 1963], pp.555–78*)*.

20. "Chosen was I to stay and you to die, You went ahead and little lost thereby" *(Goethes Werke*, vol. 1, p.380).

21. "What one desires in youth, one has in old age in plenty."

2

J.M.R. Lenz: *Der Hofmeister*

I

AFTER Goethe three other *Genies*—Lenz, Klinger, and Schiller—appear to have seized upon the theme of the split self between 1772 and 1779 as a central structural principle in one or more of their works.

Such a psychological interest can be viewed partly as a manifestation of a general development of intellectual history. Prior to the eighteenth century, unconscious phenomena and other psychological issues were generally attributed to God or the devil, and further psychological investigation was pointless. The German Enlightenment of the early eighteenth century, on the other hand, was too shallow, too preoccupied with the power of reason, to come to grips with something as psychologically subtle as the split self. But by 1770 currents of new psychological insight were pouring in upon the *Genies* from all sides. The English empiricists played a major role, and it was probably from this direction, via his teacher Abel at the *Karlsschule*, that Schiller derived the idea of what is now termed "psychosomatic illness."

H.W. von Gerstenberg, for example, conveyed in *Ugolino* (1768) a strong suggestion of an Oedipal problem. Here he permits the one son to escape from the tower in which father and brothers are imprisoned to seek out—in an unmistakable atmosphere of forbidden pleasure—his mother, held captive in a secluded room. The *Genies* were not the only ones open to such unconscious material. In *Minna von Barnhelm* (1767), G.E. Lessing had already achieved, in precise and intricate manipulation of his material (as I have argued elsewhere), an astounding treatment of unconscious jealousy.

The problem of the split self, while in a larger sense a result of the psychological receptivity of the times, also required an immediate source. This was almost certainly Goethe's *Götz*, or quite likely Goethe in person, who in turn derived the idea from Herder. (The latter finally appears to have perceived it in broad terms in Shakespeare's works.)

We know that both Lenz and Klinger were overwhelmed by *Götz*, and had ample opportunity to discuss esthetic questions with its author. It is significant that, besides Schiller (who came to the theme later), precisely these two writers should have adopted the theme—if in fact they did—and that the age otherwise passed by oblivious to this esthetic development. Lenz and Klinger were Goethe's closest esthetic disciples prior to his departure for Weimar. Lenz first befriended him in Strassburg in 1771 and, like Klinger later, elicited from him a special sympathy and desire to share ideas. In 1772 Goethe was busy revising *Götz* (among other things), and Lenz was working on *Der Hofmeister*. It is not unreasonable to suppose that Lenz, if indeed he used the theme, learned about it from Goethe during this time.

It is also possible that the discussion of this problem extended beyond Goethe's inner circle to other *Genies*. At the beginning of Johann Anton Leisewitz's *Julius von Tarent* (1776)—one of the works competing for the literary prize won by Klinger's *Die Zwillinge*—Julius declares:

> Glauben Sie es, Freund, unsre Seele ist ein einfaches Wesen—hätte die Last, die diese Nacht auf der meinigen lag, ein zusammengesetztes gedrückt, die Fugen der Teile hätten nachgelassen, und der Staub hätte sich zum Staube versammelt.[1]

True to this conviction, Leisewitz's play exhibits no split self, only the simple complementarity of two inimical brothers. But the way in which this idea is formulated and its position at the outset of the play suggest a standpoint in a contemporary debate. Leisewitz may be basing his position on von Leibniz's monad theory of the soul as a unified entity. But who—if anyone—is arguing the other side of the issue? Possibly the coincidence of the theme of inimical brothers in all three of the works competing for the prize was not in fact a coincidence. It may have been the result of discussion of work in progress (as Max Rieger and Erich Schmidt suggested). If one of these three works, Klinger's *Die Zwillinge*, is based on the split self, then it is not unlikely that Leisewitz was reacting in his remark specifically to the split self as understood by the "Frankfurt school" (as Höpfner referred to it at the time)[2] centering around Goethe, Lenz, and Klinger. None of this can be established here with any degree of certainty, however, and it must be left to someone else to shed more light on the question.

In the present context, then, we will be concerned with two main questions in examining *Der Hofmeister:* Is the work concerned with the split self and, if so, does textual evidence establish a connection to *Götz?* Secondly, what further insight does this perspective afford into the work? Elsewhere Lenz says nothing to support the idea that he was aware of the split self in *Götz.* His exultant praise of Goethe's play centers on the concepts of freedom and action:

> Das lernen wir daraus, daß diese unsre handlende Kraft nicht eher ruhe, nicht eher ablasse zu wirken, zu regen, zu toben, als bis sie uns Freiheit um uns her verschafft, Platz zu handeln: Guter Gott Platz zu handeln und wenn es ein Chaos wäre das du geschaffen, wüste und leer, aber Freiheit wohnte nur da. . . .[3]

While the theme of freedom or emancipation is one of the basic elements of the split-self problem here, it is too general, in itself, to be of significance in the context of establishing an influence of *Götz* on *Der Hofmeister*—and all the more so since Goethe did not emphasize that aspect of the emancipated personality.

II

Unlike Klinger, who at first was anxious to gather up esthetic ideas wherever he found them, Lenz, despite his desperate attempts to follow literally in Goethe's footsteps, was inwardly struggling with problems that could not be solved by extrapolating his esthetics entirely from his gifted friend. Lenz was fundamentally inner-directed, and the lines of influence from external sources tended to dissolve at the boundaries of his own sphere, to be taken up only on his own terms and in the context of his own concerns. Even his comment on *Götz* betrays a desperation more characteristic of his own inner state than of Goethe's play. Lenz sought his own answers to esthetic and philosophical questions, not so much in a pedantic playing with ideas as in the attempt to create his own reality from them, to impose order, synthesis, and rationality upon his world. It was in this sense that he insisted on the utmost realism as a medium in which a practical model of society could be created. He attempted to unite this outward-looking social perspective with the values of his introverted pietism, and sought a framework to deal with human feelings and suffering:

> Von jeher und zu allen Zeiten sind die Empfindungen, Gemütsbewegungen und Leidenschaften der Menschen auf ihre Religionsbegriffe gepfropft, ein Mensch ohne alle Religion hat gar keine Empfindung (weh ihm!, ein Mensch mit schiefer Religion schiefe Empfindungen und ein Dichter, der die Religion seines Volkes nicht gegründet hat, ist weniger als ein Meßmusikant. . . . Du [poet] sollst mir keinen Menschen auf die Folter bringen, ohne zu sagen, warum.[4]

In view of the tenor of such concerns we would not expect Lenz to borrow the theme of the split self unless it conformed and contributed to his effort to bridge the gap between his threatened inner world and the outer reality of society.

The action of *Der Hofmeister* (1774) is divided into two

intersecting plots: Fritz von Berg leaves home and his beloved cousin Gustchen in order to study in Leipzig with his
childhood friend Pätus. Gustchen, meanwhile, makes love to
her tutor, the title figure Läuffer. She becomes pregnant, and
both flee the wrath of her father, the crude and violent Major
von Berg. Läuffer finds refuge with the pastor and schoolmas-
ter Wenzeslaus. He subsequently castrates himself out of
guilt and despair, falls in love with a young girl, and the two
make plans to marry, despite his condition. Meanwhile Pätus,
already destitute and alienated from his father, makes a girl
pregnant. Fritz forces him to mend his ways, managing to
bring Pätus and himself, Pätus' girl friend and Gustchen,
along with their respective fathers, together in a joyous reconciliation.

Up to a certain point, the text provides obvious suggestions
of a split-self theme. The action revolves around four
variations of the father-son conflict, and at least three of these
reflect Lenz's own life. Like the title-figure Läuffer, Lenz
himself was the son of a pastor, and had been a *Hofmeister*.
Like Fritz von Berg and Pätus, he became estranged from his
father when he ran off to study in Strassburg. In general the
deep anxiety of his own circumstances, leading to madness
and early death, is well reflected in the atmosphere of the
play, particularly in respect to Läuffer. Even the moments of
pure comedy betray a certain hysteria peculiar to, and expressive of, Lenz. Beyond Lenz's underlying but external
biographical unification of his characters, a distinct logic
connects them within the play and supplies an inner structure
and coherence for what might superficially appear to be an
arbitrary, paper doll-like multiplication of father-son relationships. Albrecht Schöne has provided a fruitful analysis of the
underlying motif of the Prodigal Son.[5] The theme provides
the foundation for Lenz's treatment of what appears to be the
split self.

To begin with, four stages of self align themselves, for the
most part, along a temporal axis. Young Leopold, son of the
major, is the earliest—a pure example of the effect of paternal
oppression. Indeed, he is damned by his crude father to
become an ugly product without hope of escape or salvation.

But Leopold hardly appears on stage and cannot be considered on an equal basis with the other son figures. His tutor is Läuffer, older, capable of obsequious social graces, but, like Leopold, bound to the house and authority of the major. A third stage (although presumably younger than Läuffer) is Fritz von Berg, son of the *Geheimer Rat* and nephew of the major. Fritz at least emancipates himself from home when he leaves to study in Leipzig. A connection among these three is subtly suggested when the major voices his concern that Leopold might follow after his cousin Fritz:

. . . daß ein Galgendieb aus Dir geworden ist, wie der junge Hufeise oder wie Deines Onkels Friedrich, eh Du mir so ein Gassenläuferischer Taugenichts—ich will Dich zu Tode hauen—. . . .[6]

The term "Gassenläuferisch" contains a suggestion of Läuffer. (The meaning is opposed to the suggestion of servitude in the name, but from the major's twisted perspective as an oppressive father, such a contradictory sense is perfectly appropriate). As a possible third stage of four selves, Fritz is torn between emancipation, a kind of exile depriving him of love, and his inner feelings, which draw him back to his father and to the major's daughter Gustchen. Thus he can be regarded as a balance between the two states—partly emancipated but still capable of love, although separated from its object. Consequently, pending a resolution of these opposing tendencies, he does not fully possess either emancipation or love. His old friend Pätus, finally, is more radically emancipated, neither yearning to return home like Fritz (at least not initially) nor capable of love. Instead, he indulges in a jaded, cynical pursuit of erotic adventure.

It is above all in Pätus that the temporal and developmental dimension of the son figures comes into focus, particularly in relation to Fritz. From Pätus' point of view—according to our expectations from the general hypothesis for the theme— Fritz should seem childishly tied to his family milieu: "Ey was, Berg! Du bist ja kein Kind mehr, daß du nach Papa und Mama—Pfuy Teufel!" (2.3.p.60)[7] He sees Fritz as intellectually inferior: "Du wirst mich doch nicht zwingen wollen; einfältiger Mensch—" (4.6.p.97).[8] Like Mephisto, Pätus is surrounded by the nimbus of the devil. While not directly equated with such a figure, he is associated with expressions containing the word and frequently uses it himself. In exhibiting a certain quality of helpless ruin, of having abused and wasted earlier positive energies and virtues, Pätus anticipates the more extreme artist figures of Wedekind. He is described as having fallen from a gallows (2.3.p.62) and as a "hanged Pätus" (2.7.p.70). Pätus is a Prodigal Son (2.7.p.72). In anticipation of Kafka's *Landarzt*, fleeing at the end of the novella with his furs waving from the wagon, Pätus, dressed in furs, runs from the village dogs (2.4.pp.65-66). Pätus must wear furs in the summer heat because he cannot obtain money from his father to recover his clothes from the tailor; i.e., he cannot survive in total emancipation. As a result, he visibly and publicly becomes an object of laughter and ridicule. Dogs also abound in the terms used to describe him. This scene suggests that the extreme of emancipation, with a radical severance from the father, literally leads to the dogs. In any case Pätus' complete ruin and ridicule prepare the way for the retraction of this extreme personality through a change in character.

As the plot nears resolution Pätus seems to be resolved into Fritz. Even at the beginning Fritz is seen as having "power over" Pätus to make "something proper out of him" (2.3.p.62). If the scene with the village dogs symbolically demonstrates Pätus' psychological bankruptcy, a more concrete consequence soon follows in the form of debtor's prison. But Fritz, consistent with his function as the less emancipated of the two, offers to take his place in jail while Pätus attempts to scrape some money together. The problem of money is crucial to the emancipated self. Like Wedekind's Keith, Pätus not only lacks money but seems unable to hold onto it, even when he has some. This clearly reflects the Prodigal Son, who squandered his inheritance.

It is reasonable to ask whether this particular detail, so important in the literature of the split self, does not also carry a deeper significance (one which, for that matter, may be inherent in the Biblical story as well). According to C.G. Jung, the early alchemists understood gold (so close to *Geld* both in function and phonetics) as a symbol of love or psychic energy.[9] Ilse A. Graham has analyzed the symbolism of the giving and receiving of money, or the failure to do so, in *Minna von Barnhelm* in terms of love or the failure to love. This is the one work Lenz singles out for praise in *Der Hofmeister*.[10] Such a significance, if justified, would inextricably tie the problem of emancipation and inability to love to the Biblical theme as Lenz understood it.

Whatever the source and significance of Pätus' financial problems, his situation and characteristics fit precisely those the theory predicts for the emancipated son: jaded cynicism, total independence, poverty, and a callous treatment of the opposite sex. But the natural, downward course of events for the emancipated personality is suddenly reversed when Pätus wins a lottery, frees Fritz from prison, and repays the debt to their respective fathers. When, following this, Fritz takes the side of the cowardly Rehaar (whose daughter Pätus has compromised), demanding satisfaction from Pätus and forcing a showdown with his cynical personality, Pätus backs down, suddenly reforms, and nobly allows Rehaar to wound him without defending himself. Fritz now steps in to support his friend. Thus the two are joined—but not in a synthesis. Pätus accepts Fritz's values completely, becoming virtually indistinguishable from him in character. Similarly the brutish major, stricken with anguish over the disappearance of Gustchen (who is desperate over her pregnancy), is broken in spirit. The *Geheimer Rat*, Fritz's father, steps in to dictate the proper paternal attitude at the end. This includes the rehabilitation of the elder Pätus who now regrets that he drove his blind mother from his door.

While the temporal, developmental sequence seems logical and consistent, it does not in itself establish the split self in the literal sense with which we are concerned. The issues of the ability to love and the oppression by the father are reasonably clear, but these themes in themselves also do not establish that the various son figures are to be understood as complementary parts of a single psychic whole. Lenz may have viewed his main characters simply as alternatives, testing each for his ability to survive. Nevertheless a few passages specifically point to a unity of self. At the beginning the major refers—indeed artificially—to Fritz as his brother's *only* son (1.2.p.42). Shortly after this, we hear a discussion of whether the *second* son of the *Geheimer Rat* should join Leopold as a source of additional income for Läuffer (2.1.p.57). If Lenz made use of this clear discrepancy to hint at an underlying unity, then one would expect additional textual evidence to carry out the idea. While such evidence is forthcoming, it is vague and uncertain. One passage ties Fritz to Pätus in a manner reminiscent of Götz and Weislingen:

> Ich hab' ihn von Jugend auf gekannt: wir haben uns noch niemals was abgeschlagen. Er hat mich wie seinen Bruder geliebt, ich ihn wie meinen. Als er nach Halle reiste, weint' er zum erstenmal in seinem Leben, weil er nicht mit mir reisen konnte. (2.7.p.71)[11]

Pätus' landlady suggests a blood relationship (2.3.p.62). Pätus' difficulties are directly associated with his separation from Fritz: ". . . und doch wollt es das Schicksal und unsre Väter so, daß wir nicht zusammen reissten und das war sein Unglück" (2.7.p.71).[12] In a subtler suggestion of unity Major von Berg rages about Fritz to the latter's father in a manner unrealistic even for a man of his temperament, unless Fritz is viewed on a certain level as his own son: "Schreib ihm zurück: sie sollen ihn hängen" (4.1.p.85).[13]

At the end Fritz and Pätus are strangely equated when, at the arrival of the major, the *Geheimer Rat* announces in the plural: "Weißt Du was Neues, Major? Es finden sich Freyer für Deine Tochter—" (5.12.p.119).[14] Only Fritz is courting Gustchen; Pätus is wooing Rehaar's daughter. But the two girls, for their part, are also unified at the home of the *Geheimer Rat:* "Hier, Gustchen, bring ich Dir eine Gespielin. Ihr seyd in *einem*, Alter, *einem* Verhältnisse—Gebt Euch die Hand und seyd Freundinnen." (5.7.p.106)[15]

Fritz is also identified with Läuffer when he emphatically declares that the entire blame for Gustchen's situation, i.e., her pregnancy by Läuffer, rests with himself (presumably because he did not return to her soon enough): "Schuldig war ich; einzig und allein schuldig." (5.11.p.117)[16]

III

Much of this evidence is tenuous and could be accounted for on some other basis, while the least ambiguous passages are too scattered to enable us to speak with confidence of a split self in consequential dramatic realization. In his *Anmerkungen übers Theater*, written over the same period as *Der Hofmeister*, Lenz may have expressed his reasons for leaving this theme somewhat vague. In one passage he suggests that his creative method is a matter of subtle "brush strokes":

> Werd ich gelesen und der Kopf ist so krank oder so klein, daß alle meine Pinselzüge unwahrgenommen vorbeischwimmen, geschweige in ein Gemälde zusammenfließen—Trost! ich wollte nicht gelesen werden.[17]

Elsewhere in his essay he rails against what he considers to be the French tradition of destroying nature in the imposition of poetic structure. For this reason he may well have hesitated to turn his work into a psychological allegory. Nature must be present in an unadulterated form, as a work of art in itself, he argues, without the need for the artist's interference, at least not in the surrealistic way the split self seems to require. Nevertheless he recognizes the work of art as the expression of the artist's own personality: "Ich sage, der Dichter malt das ganze Stück auf seinem eigenen Charakter" (p.737).[18] And yet he regrets this too:

> So sehr er [Rousseau] abändert, so geschickt er sich unter die Personen zu verstecken weiß, die er auftreten läßt, so guckt doch immer, ich kann es nicht leugnen, etwas von seiner Perücke hervor, und das wünscht' ich weg, um mich ganz in seine Welt hineinzutäuschen, . . . (P.737)[19]

Lenz seems to be seeking an esthetic theory between two basic and conflicting standpoints. On the one hand is the imitation of nature without the meddling interjection of the poet's personality:

> Ich suchte Trost in den sogenannten Charakterstücken, allein ich fand so viel Aehnlichkeit mit der Natur (und noch weniger) als bei den Charaktermasken auf einem Ball. Ihr ganzer Vorzug bleibe also der Bau der Fabel, die willkürliche Zusammensetzung der Begebenheiten, zu welcher Schilderei der Dichter seine eigene Gemütsverfassung als den Grund unterlegt. Sein ganzes Schauspiel (ich rede hier von Meisterstücken) wird also nicht ein Gemälde der Natur, sondern seiner eigenen Seele. Und da haben wir oft nicht die beste Aussicht zu hoffen. (P.736)[20]

On the other hand, he compares the poet to God in his Creation, and the unity of the poetic creation to an apparently pietist-mystical unity of God in nature:

> Der Dichter und das Publikum müssen die eine Einheit fühlen aber nicht klassifizieren. Gott ist nur Eins in allen seinen Werken, und der Dichter muß es auch sein, wie groß oder klein sein Wirkungskreis auch immer sein mag. (P.730)[21]

Here, then, is not only the same concept of the poet as the unifying principle behind his characters, as Herder expressed it, but the additional requirement that the public feel (but not "classify") this unity. This qualification stems from the fact that the poetic work, while a creation of the poet, also forms a part of nature as the creation of God. The poet must respect this natural integrity of his material at the same time as he organizes it around himself.[22] Perhaps significantly, in the same broad terms with which Herder expounded the unity of Shakespeare in his works, Lenz is expressing a similar unity of the poet's self in his work, as well as the need to disguise this unity, so that it may be felt but not consciously analyzed.

While the textual evidence for the split self in *Der Hofmeister* is suggestive, but inconclusive, we can summarize the larger context of evidence as follows: (a) a possible and feasi-

ble influence of Goethe or *Götz* as a source for the theme, but
without clear biographical or textual evidence for such an
influence; (b) a broad range of interrelationships among the
various characters that suggest a unity of self but also may be
interpreted as a series of alternative selves; (c) a few direct
hints of a unity of self in the text that may be difficult to
account for on some other basis, but insufficient in themselves to establish the theme; (d) a psychological division
between oppressed childhood and impoverished emancipation, based at least in part on the theme of the Prodigal Son
and fulfilling with precision the expectations from our
psychological hypothesis; and (e) Lenz's own general statement of a unity of the poet's self in his work, including his
reason for disguising this unity, so that it may be felt but not
consciously analyzed.

IV

In its entirety the evidence is at least highly suggestive of a
split self. A closer look at the constellation of the four son
figures from this point of view reveals that the key to the
underlying emotional content of the play is Läuffer. As the
plot resolves itself toward a comic denouement, the characters
also seem to resolve themselves, as we have seen, into one
son (Fritz), one father (the *Geheimer Rat*), and one daughter
(Gustchen). But this happy end does not include Läuffer, or
only superficially appears to include him. Since both he and
the young, naive Lise reject Wenzeslaus' objections to their
marriage, it is superficially implied that they will marry, in a
separate but equal finale to the weddings of Fritz and Gustchen, Pätus and Rehaar's daughter. Karl Guthke speaks here
of Läuffer's "Tragik (deren radikale Konsequenz dann durch
den versöhnenden Schluß plötzlich abgebogen wird)".[23] But
Läuffer's tragedy is by no means averted. It is blacked out,
ominously truncated—yet it is totally certain.[24] The last we
hear of him is that he only needs to secure the approval of
Lise's parents to marry her, despite the pastor's objections.
Even if such approval were forthcoming—which would be

highly unlikely—the marriage would still be catastrophic,
regardless of the present unconcern of an underaged fiancée.
Läuffer's tragic fate could not be more clearly prepared,
even if it remains unrealized on the stage. We should consider
what it means in relationship to the other characters, whose
reconciliation is now completely separated from him. Läuffer
has close ties to each of the other son figures. Like Leopold
he is tied to the major's brutality; like Fritz he becomes
Gustchen's "Romeo" (as she calls them both); and like Pätus
he makes a girl pregnant. Läuffer in fact systematically experiences their disadvantages; chiefly oppression and sexual
guilt. His escape to Wenzeslaus brings no freedom, but only a
humbling routine of duties barely sufficient for physical survival:

> *Wenzeslaus.* Ey was Freyheit! Ich bin auch so frey nicht; ich
> bin an meine Schule gebunden, und muß Gott und meinem
> Gewissen Rechenschaft von geben. (3.4.p.81)[25]

If Läuffer initially shares the ability to love characteristic of
the oppressed son, this ability is for him a source of moral
anguish. And if Pätus represents an emancipated self incapable of love, then Läuffer's self-emasculation places him in a
similar, if more radical, condition. It is not unreasonable,
therefore, to conclude that Läuffer underlies the entire range
of the remaining son figures. His dark words, "Ich muß sehen,
wie ich das elende Leben zu Ende bringe, weil mir doch der
Tod verboten ist—"(2.2.p.60)[26], carry more weight than the
operatic reconciliation of the others.

Läuffer's tragic situation subtly penetrates the harmless
romantic comedy of the work, as well as its satirical grotes-
queries, with an anguished and bitter undertone of self-denial
and self-destruction. Läuffer is indeed the central figure, as
the title suggests. He represents a significant second, private
level of the play. As Burger notes (*op.cit.*, p.65), the happy
end is theater for the superficial entertainment of the audience. Perhaps it is also a kind of vicarious salvation for Lenz.
In the Berlin manuscript of the play he designated his work a
"Comedy and Tragedy," and a passage from *Anmerkungen*

übers Theater suggests how he viewed these two dimensions of the emotional atmosphere:

> Denn der Held allein [in tragedy] ist der Schlüssel zu seinen Schicksalen. Ganz anders ists mit der Komödie. Meiner Meinung nach wäre immer der Hauptgedanke einer Komödie eine Sache, einer Tragödie eine Person. . . . Die Personen [in comedy] sind für die Handlungen da—für die artigen Erfolge, Wirkungen, Gegenwirkungen, ein Kreis herumgezogen, der sich um eine Hauptidee dreht—und es ist eine Komödie. . . . Im Trauerspiele aber sind die Handlungen um der Person willen da—sie stehen nicht in meiner Gewalt, . . . (P.744)[27]

Here, then, Lenz resolves the conflict between the poet's manipulation of his material and the requirement of its natural integrity by separating these two aspects according to *genre.* The Fritz-Pätus plot is romantic comedy, fully manipulated around a "central idea" (of the split self?) while the underlying and unifying Läuffer identity, despite comic strains and a superficial suggestion of comic resolution, is the subject of tragic character and lies outside Lenz's power to manipulate.

Der Hofmeister is a work of great originality and in some ways even greater emotional power and subtlety than *Götz.* Although it is not entirely certain whether Lenz was influenced by Goethe's treatment of the split self, his own treatment of the underlying psychological problem illuminates a common archetypal ground. In both works a childhood is juxtaposed to an adult emancipation, with erotic and guilt-laden sexuality. Beyond this, everything else is strikingly different. In *Götz* the childhood is looked back upon as possessing love and genius, while only the damnation of paternal oppression is found in Lenz's Leopold. Where Goethe's portrayal of Weislingen largely as his present, emancipated self is (psychologically speaking) harshly realistic, Lenz's positive resolution of Pätus into the ideally balanced Fritz represents a conscious, ironically willful, comic manipulation. Lenz was too desperate not to attempt to create a poetic reality to counter his own circumstances. He was also too serious a poet not to bring these circumstances along into his created world in an attempt to master them. Where he ultimately failed in the one world, he succeeded impressively in the other.

Notes

1. "Believe it, friend, our soul is a unified entity—if the burden which lay on mine last night had pressed on a composite soul, the joints of the parts would have yielded and the whole thing would have turned to dust." (J. A. Leisewitz, *Julius von Tarent*, in *Sturm und Drang: Dramatische Schriften*, ed. Erich Loewenthal and Lambert Schneider, 2 vols., [Heidelberg: Verlag Lambert Schneider, n.d.], 1:557).

2. Max Rieger, *Klinger in der Sturm- und Drangperiode*. (Darmstadt: Arnold Bergstrasser, 1880), p.83.

3. "We learn from it that our power to act does not rest, does not cease to work, to excite, to rage, until it has created freedom around us, room to act: Good God room to act, and even if it were chaos which you had created, desolate and empty, but only freedom resided there." (J. M. R. Lenz, *Werke und Schriften*, ed. Britta Titel and Helmut Haug, 2 vols. [Stuttgart: Goverts Neue Bibliothek der Weltliteratur, 1966], 1:379).

4. "In all ages the senses, emotions and passions of humans are supported by their religious beliefs, a person without any religion has no sensibilities (alas for him!), a person with a twisted religion has twisted sensibilities, and a poet who has not fathomed the religion of his people is less than a church musician. . . . You [poet] should not bring a person to torture without saying why." (*Anmerkungen übers Theater*, in *Sturm und Drang: Kritische Schriften* [Heidelberg: Verlag Lambert Schneider, 1963],p.742).

5. Albrecht Schöne, *Säkularisation als sprachbildende Kraft* (Studien zur Dichtung deutscher Pfaffersöhne, Palaestra, no. 226; Göttingen: Vandenhoeck und Ruprecht, 1958).

6. " . . . that a gallows thief has become of you, like the young Hufeise or like your uncle's Friedrich, before you [become] such a street-wise bum—I'll beat you to death—" (J. M. R. Lenz, *Gesammelte Werke in vier Bänden*, ed. Richard Daunicht, 4 vols. [Munich: Wilhelm Fink, 1967], 1:121). All quotations from *Der Hofmeister* are taken from this edition.

7. "O, Berg! After all you aren't a child any more that you . . . to Papa and Mama—what the devil!"

8. "You won't want to force me; simpleton—"

9. C. G. Jung, *Psychologie und Alchemie* (Zurich: Rascher Verlag, 1944).

10. Ilse Appelbaum-Graham, "The Currency of Love: A Reading of Lessing's *Minna von Barnhelm*," *German Life and Letters* 18 (1964): 270–78.

11. "I've known him from childhood: we have never refused anything to one another. He has loved me like his brother, I've loved him like mine. When he went to Halle he cried for the first time in his life because he couldn't go with me."

12. "And yet fate and our fathers did not want us to travel together, and that was his downfall."

13. "Write him back: they should hang him."

14. "Want to hear something new, Major? There are suitors for your daughter—"
15. *"Geheimer Rat.* Here, Gustchen, I am bringing you a playmate, you are the same age, in the same condition—shake hands and be friends."
16. "I was guilty; solely and alone guilty."
17. "If I am read and the head is so sick or so small that all my brushstrokes swim by unperceived, much less flow together into a painting—No problem! I'd rather not be read." *(Anmerkungen übers Theater, op. cit.,* p.732).
18. "I say the poet paints the whole piece from his own character."
19. "As much as he [Rousseau] changes, as skillfully as he hides himself among the characters he has appear, there is still always something of his wig peeking out, I can't deny it, and I'd like to see it gone in order to enter totally into the illusion of his world . . . ."
20. "I sought comfort in the so-called character plays, but I found as much similarity to nature (and less) as in the character masks at a ball. Their entire advantage thus remains the construction of the plot, the wilful coincidence of the events, for the description of which the poet inserts as a basis his own mental state. His entire play (I'm speaking here of masterworks) thus becomes a painting not of nature but of his own soul. And there we often don't have the best of prospects."
21. "The poet and the public must feel this one unity but not classify it. God is only One in all of his works, and the poet must be the same, as large or small as his province may be."
22. Cf. Heinz Otto Burger's discussion of this point ("J. M. R. Lenz: *Der Hofmeister,"* in *Das deutsche Lustspiel,* vol. 1, ed. Hans Steffen [Kleine Vandenhoeck-Reihe, no. 271S; Göttingen: Vandenhoeck und Ruprecht, 1968], pp. 53–54.
23. " . . . tragedy (the radical consequence of which is then suddenly averted by the reconciliatory ending)" (Karl S. Guthke, "Nachwort" to *Der Hofmeister* [Universalbibliothek, no. 1376; Stuttgart: Reclam Verlag, 1966],p.94).
24. This has gone generally unremarked or unrecognized. Edward P. Harris, for example ("Structural Unity in J. M. R. Lenz's *Der Hofmeister:* A Revaluation," *Seminar, 8* [June, 1972], 77–87) refers to Läuffer's final "ideal fulfillment of love in being loved and accepted for himself" (p.86). One of few to see through the thin veneer of a comic, positive resolution of Läuffer's fate is Rene Girard, who at least recognizes it as absurd: " . . . ce dénouement factice est en rę une démonstration par l 'absurde, un dernier commentaire du cas Läuffer" (*Lenz 1751–1792: Genese d'une Dramaturgie du Tragi-comique* [Paris: Librairie C. Klincksieck, 1968],p.280). Somewhat less emphatically, Helmut Arntzen has labeled this comic resolution a "parody" of the comedy of the Enlightenment (*Die ernste Komödie: das deutsche Lustspiel von Lessing bis Kleist* [Sammlung Dialog; Munich: Nymphenburger Verlagshandlung, 1968],p.90).
25. *"Wenzeslaus.* Freedom you say! I'm not so free, either; I'm tied to my school and have to answer to God and my conscience."
26. "I must see how I can bring this miserable life to an end; after all, death is forbidden to me—"
27. "For the hero alone (in tragedy) is the key to his fate. It's entirely different in comedy. In my opinion the main idea of a comedy is always a thing, in a tragedy it is a person. . . . The characters [in comedy] are there for the plot, a circle around it which revolves around a central idea—and it is a comedy. . . . In tragedy however the plot is there for the sake of the person—it is not subject to my control."

3

F.M. Klinger: *Die Zwillinge*

I

FRIEDRICH Maximilian Klinger openly imitated both Goethe's *Götz* (in *Otto*, 1775) and Lenz's *Hofmeister* (in *Das leidende Weib*, 1775). He used numerous character names and recreated similar external circumstances. In neither play, however, did he include any suggestions of a split self. One would suppose that he, like almost everyone else, saw nothing of the sort in either source, that his imitations were only shallow and slightly baroque echoes with their brooding pathos and stark moral polarities.

And yet, immediately after these first attempts he wrote *Die Zwillinge* (written in the summer of 1775 and published in 1776). Here a split self clearly dominates dialogue and action. As we have discussed in connection with Lenz, Klinger most likely became acquainted with the theme through direct personal contact with Goethe, either in May of 1775 or possibly during the preceding Christmas vacation. Such a personal influence would explain why Klinger, so quick to absorb new sources, should have waited until this time to adopt the theme. Apparently, he hadn't recognized it by himself, but only after Goethe told him about it.[1]

Placed in Italy, the drama centers upon Guelfo, the younger of twins, who resents the inheritance and generally loved and favored status of his brother Ferdinando, whom he considers to be cowardly and deceitfully ingratiating in his pleasant manners. Ferdinando arrives home in preparation for his wedding the next day to Kamilla, whom Guelfo also desires. The spare action focuses on Guelfo's brooding dialogue with his confidante Grimaldi, the efforts of parents, Kamilla and Ferdinando to assuage his black mood, and his murder of Ferdinando on a horseback ride. The play ends with a confrontation between Guelfo and his family and his execution by the father. The language and atmosphere of the work are surrealistically ambiguous and darkly symbolic.

It is not certain that Klinger reacted to the split-self theme in *Der Hofmeister* as a source, although if he in fact learned of it from Goethe, it is unlikely that either he or Goethe would have failed to recognize it in Lenz's play. But only two motifs point to this source: a single reference to the Prodigal Son[2] and three references to an only son (3.1.p.288; 4.5.p.312; 5.1.p.316), where two sons coexist:

> *Amalia.* Nein, nicht! Mein Einziger und jetzt mein Einziger thats nicht! (5.1.p.316)[3]

This motif receives even more emphasis in Guelfo's description of a violent family scene:

> Und sie alle netzten Ferdinando mit Tränen, schrien, als hätt ich sie an der Gurgel: "Einziger, rette uns!" —Merkst du das Wort? Einziger! Wie viel darinnen liegt! (3.1.p.288)[4]

Thus the family appeals to Ferdinando to act as a whole person; i.e., with a unified will and commitment reflecting a reintegration of the self. If Klinger did in fact borrow these two motifs from Lenz, it does not appear that he intended anything like the public indebtedness of *Das leidende Weib.* Similarly, the only possible specific influence of the split self in *Götz* is a general resemblance of Ferdinando to Weislingen, and that is by no means proof of an influence. Like Götz's alter ego, Ferdinando is characterized by a high degree of socialization and is regarded by his counterpart as having abdicated inner integrity. Like Weislingen, Ferdinando also possesses the desirable woman. Guelfo, for his part, is a *Kraftmensch*, as is Götz. But here the similarities end. After openly following Goethe and Lenz in his first two works, Klinger may have felt obliged in *Die Zwillinge*—where a deeper-lying and more significant dependency or at least similarity can be demonstrated—to cover his tracks.[5] While this remains speculation, in any case the circumstances of the play's conception speak strongly for Goethe's direct personal influence. Goethe was deeply involved in helping his impoverished friend establish himself as a dramatist, and the two were together shortly before *Die Zwillinge* was written.

The only recognition of the split-self theme in the Klinger literature (so far as I have been able to determine) appears to consist of a few comments by Gert Mattenklott. Focusing on Grimaldi as a carrier of backward-looking, undramatic melancholy, and Guelfo as the forward-looking, dramatic figure, Mattenklott observes that a separation is necessitated by the contradiction between these two attitudes:

> Dennoch wird Grimaldi in die Handlung integriert, denn: in der Reflexion auf sich selbst wird das Leiden an der Spaltung der Person deutlich, die sich in Treue zur Vergangenheit und Erfüllung der Forderung der Gegenwart zu teilen hat.[6]

But Mattenklott does not pursue this idea in the direction of the split self.

II

The text itself provides sufficient evidence for an adequate understanding of the split self as Klinger develops it. The central, dominant part of the self is Guelfo. More than in *Götz* or in *Der Hofmeister* the perception of the world of the play emanates from this one figure. Basically Guelfo is an amoral, almost infantile *Kraftmensch*. This condition supposedly has arisen from the injustice of a system giving Ferdinando the family lands, when his status as first-born of twins makes little sense and is in fact uncertain—at least in Guelfo's mind (1.2.p.244). Guelfo's main impulse, like that of so many of Klinger's early protagonists, is revenge (3.1.p.290). At the same time he sees himself as the Prodigal Son (1.4.p.257)—a figure of emancipation that actually contradicts his home-bound and regressive characteristics. The apparent illogic of associating this motif with Guelfo further suggests Klinger's tendency to vacuum up motifs where he found them.

In any case Guelfo, as the dominant figure boiling with energy and will, is close to uniting the whole self. When Grimaldi plays alternately gentle and violent passages on the piano, Guelfo fears that his soul will depart from his body. He is able, in speaking of himself in the third person, to imply more than one personality in himself:

> Dich und Dein Instrument in die Tiber, Schwärmer! Was willst Du mich locken, daß meine Seele auf diesen Saiten schwebe? Daß ich den Guelfo vergesse? (1.1.p.238)[7]

Preparing for the murder of his brother, Guelfo is tormented by guilt and tries to tear himself out of himself:

> Ha! ich kann mich nicht ansehen! Reiß dich aus dir, Guelfo! *(zerschlägt den Spiegel)* zerschlage dich, Guelfo!—Guelfo! geh aus dir! Schaff dich um! (4.4.p.310)[8]

The word "umschaffen" suggests a desired remodeling of character, if not necessarily a yielding to the personality of Ferdinando.

Guelfo dominates Grimaldi, the second of three part selves. Grimaldi is perhaps better understood as a subsplit within Guelfo. This creates an atmosphere of soliloquy in the discussions between the two, rather than a dialog between coequals. Grimaldi does not oppose Guelfo, like Ferdinando, but shares his hatred and desire for revenge (1.1.p.240). He is also described, like Guelfo, as "violent" (2.1.p.259). He acknowledges his unity with Guelfo: "Uns wirft das Unglück zusammen, und kettet uns fest an. Wir wollen uns näher rücken" (3.1.p.285).[9]

Although not a member of the family, Grimaldi addresses Guelfo's father as "Vater" (2.3.p.273;4.3.p.306). Despite his similarity, devotion, and subservience to Guelfo, strengthen-ing the latter in the struggle against Ferdinando, Grimaldi also poses a threat. Through the implication of their unity he weakens Guelfo by yearning for sleep—a tendency that represents a certain lameness or paralysis (2.1.p.260). When the two compare themselves to Cassius and Brutus, Guelfo chooses the former and Grimaldi the latter. Grimaldi would prefer to give up existence altogether:

> Laß uns zusammen sitzen und absterben, wie der Fisch, dem das Wasser abgeleitet ist. So ists nun. Nicht zu seyn, Guelfo! nicht zu seyn mehr! (3.1.p.289)[10]

Thus Guelfo has some reason to fear his friend, and when the latter recoils before him after the murder, then seizes him tightly, Guelfo senses that Grimaldi has joined Ferdinando against him:

> *Guelfo.* Du hältst mich immer fester—Deine Hand wird immer feuriger—Hast Du den Bund mit ihm gemacht? Ist sein Geist in Dich gefahren? (4.5.p.312)[11]

Guelfo's description of the murder scene suggests that he originally had expelled Ferdinando from himself and now must do so once more:

> Ich will ihn herausjagen noch einmal, so sah er aus—so, so! Wie er an die Eiche sunk, rief: Bruder!—und wie ich in den Wald lachte, daß es ins Echo pfiff!—Laß mich los! Was hältst Du mich?—Bist du nicht Grimaldi, der mir gut war? (4.5.p.312)[12]

If Grimaldi represents an aspect of personality subordinate to Guelfo, then perhaps Ferdinando should be viewed in a similar fashion, since he hardly manages to get onto the stage. He is discussed, quoted, hated, loved, seen from the window, and lies dead on the stage, but otherwise has almost no immediate role of his own. From the point of view of Kamilla, Amalia, and the elder Guelfo, he represents a positive son-self. The mother Amalia urges Guelfo to let himself be led by Ferdinando's "cleverness," while the father sees this quality balanced by Guelfo's strength as a "rock in the sea" (1.4.p.252).

This could be an echo of Götz and Weislingen, as we have noted. It is also much like the complementarity of Julius and Guido in Leisewitz's competing *Julius von Tarent.* But Guelfo not only envies Ferdinando for his privileges and the love he enjoys of family and bride; he also despises his vanity (3.1.p.290) and feminine weakness (3.1.p.291). Disapproving of Ferdinando, he cannot yield to him, nor can he accept him as part of himself. The destruction of Ferdinando thus represents no new synthesis, no integration of personality. The opposite is true. The violent elimination of his opponent is a form of suicide, a collapse of personality. Guelfo therefore offers himself up for execution at the hands of the father.

III

The logic of the split among these three part selves is perhaps the one real exception, in the line of poets under discussion, to the hypothesized pattern of oppression versus emancipation. But Klinger's use of the split self almost certainly resulted from Goethe's influence and therefore should be examined here. It contains no emancipated self, incapable of love, but rather the gentle, socialized Ferdinando. As for Guelfo, there is no oppressed child, but rather an infantile megalomaniac. Beyond this dimension of socialization the logic and cause of the split are obscure. One is tempted to consider some sort of Freudian model in which Ferdinando as superego is destroyed by Guelfo as ego. However, this does not work without some problematical manipulation. If Grimaldi suggests some impoverished, inhibited part of the psyche, like the crew in Kafka's "Der Steuermann," he does not clearly represent the id, as in the latter example. Guelfo, as the dominant figure, would reasonably be seen as incorporating the ego functions. But his unsocialized, infantile rage would manifest the id as well, leaving Ferdinando as the supergo (expressing the values of the father and of society).[13] But this leaves Grimaldi still unaccounted for. He could perhaps be seen as some kind of residual reflection of the superego within Guelfo.

In the absence of some clear-cut Freudian model, as in

"Der Steuermann," such an explanation becomes dangerous-
ly willful. Then, too, Klinger could not have been thinking in
specifically Freudian terms, although he might have grasped
such relationships intuitively. In any case the text does not
provide sufficient evidence to make such a reading useful as a
basis for interpretation.

In the absence of any suggestion, past or present, of paternal oppression, the underlying father conflict of *Der Hofmeister*
(and more indirectly *Götz*) would seem to be equally
inadequate as an interpretative device here. Nor would one
expect Klinger, whose father died when he was eight, to be
interested in the problem of emancipation from the father.
And yet, it is the father who refuses to accept the whole son:

> *Ferdinando.* Mich nicht allein, mein Vater. *Alter Guelfo.* Ha!
> Dich allein! Bist Du's nicht allein, der dem Vater gütlich
> thut? (2.2.p.269)[14]

Amalia, in contrast, tries to recognize both Ferdinando and
Guelfo in one figure (1.4.p.252), while Kamilla attempts to
draw Ferdinando from Guelfo and to persuade Guelfo to be
Ferdinando (2.5.pp.276–281). But this fails and, in the end,
it is the father who executes Guelfo. A father conflict is
clearly present. This split self is not based on the father's
simple rejection of the son, as in *Der Hofmeister*. Rather, the
old Guelfo makes every attempt to love his son, so long as he
manifests the positive qualities of Ferdinando. (The situation
resembles that of the father in *Julius von Tarent*; one begins to
wonder if either Klinger or Leisewitz might have read a draft
of the other's play, prior to the completion of work.)Thus the
evil of Guelfo precedes, rather than results from, paternal
rejection. The matter of the rights of the first-born, properly
in conformance with tradition, does not, in itself, account for
Guelfo's spontaneously antagonistic personality, but only
serves as an excuse for his resentment and jealousy. Nor does
any *Kraftmensch* philosophy of the *Genies* account for his negative, evil disposition. One might simply conclude that Klinger
was not interested in the psychology of his main figure so
much as in the more immediate clash of *Kraftmensch* and
family.

Another cause for Guelfo's alienation specifically from his father suggests itself subtly in the text. When Grimaldi attempts to persuade Guelfo to join him in suicide, he holds out the hope that in death Guelfo will rejoin his beloved, deceased sister Juliette (3.1.p.289). At this point, Grimaldi then refers to his own deceased beloved and compares her to Kamilla:

> Aber Guelfo, die Gräfin! *(sieht gen Himmel)* Und dort wohnt eine, und hier wohnt sie! *(die Hand aufs Herz)* Gräfin Kamilla, Sie haben—o dieser Zug . . . das haben Sie, ja! Sie habens von ihr. . . . (2.3.pp.273–74)[15]

The elder Guelfo clarifies this relationship by identifying Grimaldi's beloved as Juliette: "*(Dazwischen vor sich)* Er meint meine Tochter, und hat Recht" (2.3.p.274).[16] This composite figure of the sister Juliette and Kamilla is then subtly combined with the mother Amalia—a procedure somewhat reminiscent of Lenz, who united figures in *Der Hofmeister.* Amalia expresses the desire of the two to join in their love for Guelfo:

> Wir zwey wollen ihn schon besänftigen. Wir wollen immer zusammen seyn; wollen ihn aufsuchen, er mag flüchten, wohin er will. O wir wollen den lieben Guelfo mit Liebe verfolgen! (4.1.p.302)[17]

Both hear the call apparently of a lover:

> *Amalia.* Mich deucht, es käme jemand geschlichen nahe zu mir. *Kamilla.* Ich hör so oft meinen Namen mit banger Stimme rufen. (4.1.p.302)[18]

The word "geschlichen" ties this passage to another, decisive one in which Amalia promises to come "geschlichen" to Guelfo in the early morning:

> O Guelfo—nicht so, morgen früh komm ich zu Dir geschlichen. Noch wenige Stunden, und die Nacht ist vorüber. (3.2.p.299)[19]

Finally, it can hardly be an accident that the name Kamilla

contains (almost) an anagramm of the name Amalia. Thus
beloved, sister, and mother are intertwined amid tones of
secret intimacy, and in a context specifically suggestive of an
ambivalent, conflict-laden response from Guelfo. The situation here parallels the overt split and conflict between Guelfo
and Ferdinando.

If this lightly but clearly suggested Oedipal-incest theme
seems a dubiously modern reading, then this is true only of
the label. The conflict itself, as we have noted, found dramatic expression in Gerstenberg's *Ugolino*. Christoph Hering has
noted echoes of *Ugolino* in Klinger's first play, *Otto*.[20] The
Oedipal conflict explains the turmoil within Guelfo, "perse-
cuted" by his mother's solicitations, as well as his specifically
infantile qualities. It also accounts for the contrasting character of Ferdinando (as a projection of characteristics within
Guelfo) specifically as socialized and lacking conflicts in his
love for Kamilla. Finally, it deepens the significance of the
father's refusal to tolerate a son-self in which such desires are
manifest.

In *Götz* the meaning of the split self was partly carried by
the parallel historical level, and directly suggested only by a
limited number of key motifs—chiefly the hand. In *Die Zwillinge*, in contrast, the inner realm of the split self is the
primary focus of the play. Klinger was therefore confronted
with the problem of manifesting the theme throughout the
text, but not letting the world of the play implode into an
abstract inner allegory. This called for a careful balance of
direct, unambiguous suggestions of the split; others that are
ambiguous; and still others that contribute to it only in de-
pendence on the first two types. But the second category of
ambiguous passages dominates, and this required a particular
esthetic effort on Klinger's part. He seems to express this in
one passage where Guelfo reacts to Grimaldi:

> Mensch! Mensch! Du machst mich rasend mit Deiner
> Zqeydeutigkeit. Merk Dir das! Wo ich Dich erwische, will
> ichs aus Dir herausziehen, und hingen die Gedanken mit
> Hacken in Deiner Seele. Du sagst zu viel und zu wenig.
> (1.1.p.240)[21]

This passage does not appear to apply to the words of Grimaldi that supposedly inspire it. It is Klinger himself who projects himself onto the stage here to comment on his own creative process. He specifically dwells on the "too much and too little" of passages that, taken symbolically, make the split self too explicit and, taken realistically, contain too little substance. The violence and destruction of Guelfo's contemplated attack on Grimaldi's soul are suggestive of the danger Klinger faced, in developing the split self, of laying bare and destroying his characters in their own world. This is much the same problem that appears to have held Lenz back from a more consequential development of the theme in *Der Hofmeister*.

IV

In a following play, *Simsone Grisaldo* (1776), Klinger undertook a somewhat different treatment of the split self. In most respects this project exaggerated the tendencies of *Die Zwillinge*. The language is even more darkly symbolic. At one point Klinger even seems to ridicule himself: "Versteh ich mich?"[22]

Instead of three-part selves, we have a total of five. A medieval Spanish king is robbed of energy, health, and prestige (1.2.p.243). He is shunted aside and ignored in favor of his magnificent General Grisaldo, who has defeated the Moors and saved the kingdom. Like his Biblical namesake, Simsone unites the promiscuously demonstrated ability to love with military prowess, and does so in the ludicrous allegorical abstract of a comic-book superman. All positive attributes have been concentrated in him. The king, in contrast, remains as a mere birthright, that is, a kind of empty seat of the ego. The remaining part-selves are the three Dons. Each represents one aspect of personality, and each envies Grisaldo and plans to usurp the throne for himself. Bastiano is reminiscent of Guelfo: grandiose and cold in his scheming and ruthless in his contempt for his opponents. However, Bastiano totally and explicitly lacks the ability to love. This quality is reserved (among the three Dons) for the poet Curio, a soft lover motivated by boundless jealousy but lacking Bastiano's courage. The last of the three, Truffaldino, is more difficult to associate with a specific characteristic. He is a close confidante of and advisor to the king; otherwise, he does not seem to possess any attribute missing in the others. Rather, Truffaldino seems to represent the king in a literal sense, perhaps as a kind of surrogate legitimacy (if that is not a contradiction in terms):

> Ich bin des Königs Rechte, des Königs Linke, des Königs Aug', des Königs Ohr, des Königs All, Dons! Mach' ihn lachen und weinen durch meine Wissenschaft. Das ganze Land fürchtet den König, der König fürchtet mich; was muß Truffaldino sein, Dons, fürcht't sich ein König vor ihm und seiner Kunst und in einem König aller Kastilier? Löst mir das Rätsel auf, Dons! (2.1.p.167)[23]

The explicit unity of these selves is frequently suggested or hinted at. Bastiano, who resembles Guelfo, berates himself in a similar fashion in dissatisfaction over his identity, then praises himself:

> Komm, Phantast! Ich will dich ausstreichen aus der Seele, neue Farben auftragen, die die Bilder reizender, wollüstiger und anziehender machen, du gefällst mir, Bastiano, so ziemlich kalt, ich bitt' dich, bleib dir getreu, oder ich jag dich aus dem morschen Bau mit Dolchstichen hinüber. (2.2.pp.186–87)[24]

The king hints of his relationship to Grisaldo:

> Was ist aus mir worden? Da lieg' ich, da bin ich zusammengefahren in mich vor Schrecken. . . . Von ihm hatte ich Leben und Kraft, . . . o mein edler Teil! (2.2.p.187)[25]

The splintering of identity is seen not as a projection of inner conflict, as in *Die Zwillinge*, but more as a result of dissolution of energies:

> *Bastiano* . . . Es ist aus! Wo sind des Menschen Kräfte? Wie steigen des Menschen Kräfte? Wie sinken des Menschen

Kräfte? Gegenwart und Zukunft, und wo durchbrechen, wo die Kette fassen und zusammenbinden und dann sagen: nun ist's! (2.2.p.190)[26]

Grisaldo indicates the subunity represented by the three Dons (complementing the situation between the king and himself): "Und wenn ich sie am Ende nicht noch alle zusammenkuppele, wie räudige Hunde ins Wasser werf, . . ."[27] Truffaldino suggests the king, however, as the final, proper locus of the whole self: "In eine Königskrone, . . fließt das Ganze zusammen (3.3.p.214)."[28] The unity of self is associated with a healthy emotional balance reminiscent of Herder's idea of healthy psychic integrity:

> *Bastiano.* Merkst du denn nicht, daß ein edles, sich fühlendes Herz keinen Schein von Teilung leiden kann. . . . (4.1.p.230)[29]

After henchmen are sent to blind Grisaldo, the three Dons usurp the crown, and Bastiano then pushes the other two aside. But Grisaldo suddenly appears (having scattered his attackers) and dismisses the three plotters. He saves the kingdom once again against a new attack by the Moors, and restores the crown to the king. The latter recognizes Bastiano's loyalty and rehabilitates his friendship with the ever selfless general:

> *König.* Ich fühl in dir und habe Stärke von dir. Denn ich fühle dein Herz wieder so ungestüm schlagen an dem meinen wie sonst. (5.3.p.257)[30]

One might best view the three Dons as projections of the unhappy king, all trying to exercise his proper qualities in the absence of actual capacities. Thus love is perverted to jealousy in Curio, *Kraft* to evil scheming in Bastiano, and legitimate rule to empty arrogance in Truffaldino:

> *König.* Es waren finstre undeutbare Bilder vor meine Seele getreten, ich war krank. Ich merk', daß der Mensch Rück-

fälle haben kann, die ihn auf eine Zeit ganz vernichten.
(5.3.p.257)[31]

Grisaldo mainly functions to carry away the virtues the king
needs for himself and finally regains by accepting Grisaldo's
friendship; i.e., by realizing himself through Grisaldo. These
suggestions are developed in the text in such a confusing and
complicated way that one suspects that Klinger was attempting to combine the split-self problem with other major
thematic material, perhaps ideas borrowed from Rousseau
and Shaftesbury.[32] Erich Schmidt aptly labeled this work as
Klinger's "most unnatural drama,"[33] and the split-self theme
with its underlying logic dispels only part of the confusion.
Despite this interesting variation on the split self, the world of
the play that only threatened to collapse in *Die Zwillinge*
appears to have done so in *Simsone Grisaldo*, and Klinger
dropped the theme.

But he returned once more to the split self in his late
novels: *Geschichte eines Teutschen aus der neusten Zeit* and *Der
Weltmann und der Dichter*. In the former, the worldly Ferdinand is contrasted with his spiritual friend Ernst. He contrib-
utes to the latter's tragic fate by making love to his wife
Amalia. The repetition of the names, along with the motif of
forbidden love—only lightly developed in *Die Zwillinge*—
helps to suggest that Klinger perceived such a theme not as a
passing experiment, but as a lasting problem. Otherwise the
identity of Ferdinand and Ernst, while reflecting two aspects
of Klinger's personality (as H.M. Waidson has noted),[34] is not
made explicitly necessary in the novel. The two main figures
can be regarded simply as complementary personalities.

The unity of the *Weltmann* and the *Dichter* is somewhat
more fundamental to the understanding of the second novel.
These two roles neatly comprise Klinger's later career, as
Christoph Hering implied in the title of his study: *F.M.
Klinger, der Weltmann und der Dichter*. Where the introverted
Ernst dominates *Geschichte eines Teutschen*, here the opposing
figure of the *Weltmann* attempts to justify his life to his
altruistic and critical poet friend. Erich Schmidt recognized
the essence of this relationship:

Klinger, endlich auf Bruderhaß und Brudermord im Drama verzichtend, versuchte zuletzt im romanhaften Dialog sein eigenes zwiespältiges Wesen in zwei Gestalten, "Dichter" und "Weltmann", ruhig auseinander zu setzen.[35]

In individual passages Klinger drops only sparse suggestions of a totality of self:

Weltmann. Ich habe, was dir mangelt; gib du mir von deinem Reichtum, und nimm von dem meinigen.[36]

Otherwise he makes no real attempt in these late works to draw structure-generating tensions and conflicts from the problem, as he had done earlier in his career.

Notes

1. Otto A. Palitzsche has argued that Guelfo's character was influenced by conversations with Goethe in connection with his work on *Egmont*, written about the same time as *Die Zwillinge (Erlebnisgehalt und Formproblem in Friedrich Maximilian Klingers Jugenddramen* [Hamburgische Texte und Untersuchungen zur deutschen Philologie, II,2; Dortmund: Ruhfus, 1924], p.52). If Goethe advised Klinger in regard to his own *Egmont*, he may also have discussed ideas realized in *Götz*. To be sure, this could not have come at the time Klinger heard of the literary competition from Miller (and presumably began work on *Die Zwillinge*), since Goethe was traveling in Switzerland. But Goethe may have discussed the relevant ideas with Klinger earlier or after his return. (Cf. Max Rieger, *Klinger in der Sturm- und Drangperiode* [Darmstadt: Arnold Bergstrasser, 1880], pp.47 – 48, 72,89,106).

2. F. M. Klinger, *Dramatische Jugendwerke*, ed. Hans Berendt and Kurt Wolff, 3 vols. [Leipzig: Ernst Rowohlt, 1912], 1:257.) All quotations from Klinger's Storm-and-Stress plays are taken from this edition.

3. "No,not! My only one and now my only one didn't do it!"

4. "And they all covered Ferdinando with tears, screamed, as though I had them by the throat: 'Only one, save us!' Do you notice that word? Only one! How much lies in it!"

5. Wilhelm Wiget found in the first scene, where Guelfo and Grimaldi are drinking wine, "eine so offensichtliche Nachahmung der Bruder Martin-Szene im Götz, daß sie dem bei der Umarbeitung längst mit Goethe zerfallenen Dichter peinlich war und deswegen [in a later reworking of *Die Zwillinge*] getilgt wurde" ("Einleitung" to *Eine unbekannte Fassung von Klingers Zwillingen* [Acta et Commentationes B 28; Tartu: K. Mattienseni, 1932],p.x.). But this similarity does not extend beyond the fact that the effects of wine are praised (differently) in both works— somewhat less than an "offensichtliche Nachahmung." Still, it is of some interest that Wiget decided that Klinger felt the need to hide his dependency on Goethe, if only later and for different reasons.

6. "Nevertheless Grimaldi is integrated into the plot, for in the reflection on himself the suffering becomes clear in the split in the person, which has to divide itself in faithfulness to the past and fulfillment of the demands of the present." [Gert Mattenklott, *Melancholie in der Dramatik des Sturm und Drang* [Studien zur allgemeinen und vergleichenden Literaturwissenschaft,1; Stuttgart: J. B. Metzlersche Verlagshandlung, 1968],p.75).

7. "You and your instrument into the Tiber, fanatic! Do you want to entice me, that my soul should float on these strings? That I should forget Guelfo?"

8. "Ha! I can't look at myself! Tear yourself out of yourself, Guelfo! *(smashes the mirror)* Smash yourself, Guelfo!—Guelfo! Go out of yourself! Change yourself!"

9. "Misfortune throws us together and chains us tightly. We want to move closer together."

10. "Let us sit together and die, like the stranded fish. So it is now. Not to be, Guelfo! Not to be any longer!"

11. "*Guelfo.* You are holding me tighter and tighter—Your hand is getting more fiery—Have you made a pact with him? Has his spirit entered you?"

12. "I want to drive him out once more, this is how he looked—thus, thus! How he sank against the oak, called: Brother!—And how I laughed into the forest, that it echoed!—Let me go! Why are you holding me?—Aren't you Grimaldi, who was nice to me?"

13. Cf. Karl S. Guthke, "F. M. Klingers *Zwillinge:* Höhepunkt und Krise des Sturm und Drang," *German Quarterly* 43 (4) November 1970): 703– 14: "Die Infantilität scheint das wesentliche, zugleich übergreifende Moment zu sein. . . . Der Held . . . gerät in Verdacht, haltloses Opfer seiner eigenen destruktiven Impulse zu sein."

14. "*Ferdinando.* Not me alone, my father. *Elder Guelfo.* Ha! You alone! Isn't it you alone, who treat your father well?"

15. "But Guelfo, the countess! *(Looks toward heaven)* And there she lives, and here she lives! *(His hand on his heart.)* Countess Kamilla, you have—oh this feature . . . you have it, yes! You have it from her."

16. "*(Aside to himself)* He means my daughter, and he is right."

17. "The two of us will calm him. We want always to be together, want to find him, wherever he may flee. O, we will persecute the dear Guelfo with love."

18. "*Amalia.* It seems to me, someone is sneaking around me. *Kamilla.* So often I hear my name called in a timid voice."

19. "O, Guelfo, not like this, tomorrow morning I'll sneak in to you. Just a few hours, and the night is over."

20. Christoph Hering, *Friedrich Maximilian Klinger: Der Weltmann als Dichter* (Berlin: DeGruyter,1966),p.46.

21. "Man! Man! You're making me crazy with your ambiguity. Note that! Where I catch you I'll pull it out of you even if the thoughts are attached to your soul with hooks. You say too much and too little."

22. *Dramatische Jugendwerke,* vol.2 (1.2,p.244).

23. "I'm the King's right hand, the King's left hand, the King's eye, the King's ear, the King's everything, Dons! I make him laugh and cry with my science. The whole land fears the King, the King fears me; what must Truffaldino be, Dons, that a King fears him and his art—and that a King of all Castilians? Solve the riddle, Dons!"

24. "*Bastiano.* Come, dreamer! I'll cross you out of the soul, bring in new colors that make the images more enticing, exciting, and attractive. I like you, Bastiano, so rather cold, I ask you, stay true to yourself, or I'll drive you out of the rotten structure to the other side with sword thrusts."

25. *"King.* What has happened to me? Here I lie, here I am withdrawn into myself from terror. . . . From him I had life and strength—o my noble part!"

26. *"Bastiano.* It's over! Where are man's powers? How do man's powers increase? How do man's powers ebb? Present and future, and where to break through, where to seize the chain and tie it together and then say: There it is!"

27. *"Grisaldo.* And if I don't tie them all together at the end, throw them into the water like mangy dogs. . . . "

28. *"Truffaldino.* The whole thing flows together . . . in a king's crown. . . . "

29. *"Bastiano.* Don't you notice that a noble, feeling heart can tolerate no appearance of division?"

30. *"King.* I feel in you and have strength from you. For I feel your heart beat against mine as strongly as before."

31. *"King.* Dark, unintelligible images had stepped in front of my soul, I was ill. I notice that the human being can have relapses that for a time destroy him entirely."

32. Cf. Luise Kolb, *Klingers Simsone Grisaldo* (Ph.D. diss., Halle, 1929); Friedrich Wyneken, *Rousseaus Einfluß auf Klinger* (University of California Publications in Modern Philology, III,1; Berkeley: University of California, 1912).

33. Erich Schmidt, *Lenz und Klinger: Zwei Dichter der Geniezeit* (Berlin: Weidemann, 1878), p.96.

34. H. M. Waidson, "Goethe and Klinger: Some Aspects of a Personal and Literary Relationship," *English Goethe Society Publications,* n.s. 23 (1953 54): 97 – 120.

35. "Klinger, finally dispensing with fraternal hate and fratricide, tried finally, in novellistic dialogue, to resolve and reconcile his own split character in two figures, 'poet' and 'statesman.' " (*Op.cit.,* p.87).

36. *"Weltmann.* I have what you lack; give me from your wealth and take from mine." (*Der Weltmann und der Dichter,* in *F. M. Klingers Sämmtliche Werke,* 9 vols. [Stuttgart and Tübingen: J. G. Cotta'scher Verlag, 1842], 9:201).

4

Friedrich Schiller: *Die Räuber*

I

The disagreement in the critical reception and evaluation of Schiller's *Die Räuber* (written 1779-1780) began when the work was first performed and persists today. Benno von Wiese has voiced the continuing critical uncertainty about the work:

> Ist dieses Drama ein verspäteter Nachkömmling der Geniezeit, gehört es in die gleiche Linie wie die Dramatik eines Lenz, Klinger, Leisewitz, wie die des jungen Goethe . . . ? Oder muß man "Die Räuber" im Zusammenhang mit der Ueberlieferung der europäischen Aufklärung sehen, unter Berufung auf den Zweck, "das Laster zu stürzen, und Religion, Moral und bürgerliche Gesetze an ihren Feinden zu rächen"? . . . Die literarhistorische Forschung hat solche Fragen bis heute noch nicht eindeutig beantworten können. Oft freilich hat sie sich in der Wertung den negativen Urteilen des 19. Jahrhunderts angeschlossen, wenn sie dem jungen Dichter jede psychologische Begabung absprach und seine Menschengestaltung unerträglich extrem und verzerrt fand.[1]

Von Wiese, up to a point, agrees with the Marxist view of the play that concerns itself with the "dialectic of social processes" (p.143). Gerhart Storz has taken issue with the interpretation of the play as a "Revolutionsdrama," seeing the real revolution in Franz's radical amorality rather than in

Karl's robber existence.[2] In an article focusing on the theme of brothers in conflict, Fritz Martini has not ignored the personal level of the play but nevertheless has systematically subordinated this to a sociological perspective—even where, as he determines for acts four and five, Schiller focuses solely on the "internal human conflicts."[3]

From the present perspective von Wiese's first alternative appears accurate: "Die Räuber" belongs in the tradition of Goethe, Lenz, and Klinger. Schiller's play, in fact, far from primarily representing a rebellion against society, culminates a central core of Storm-and-Stress plays based on the theme of the split self. The split self may well be the most important device by means of which the *Genies* realized Herder's esthetics of the poetic work as an expression of the self of its creator (as we noted in the discussion of *Götz*). Schiller's treatment of this theme is based on heavy borrowing from literary sources; indeed, his compositional genius demonstrates itself in his first play in a masterful display of synthesis.

This fact has been obscured by the seeming adequacy of the one traditionally cited source: Christian Daniel Schubart's little plot summary, "Geschichte des menschlichen Herzens." It was offered in January, 1775, in the *Schwäbisches Magazin* as a challenge to a German poet to make something out of it. Schubart's story provides the external plot: a son Carl who is alienated from his father by the devious brother's interception of correspondence, then returns in disguise to save his father from the brother's attempt to murder him. For the rest, Schubart's Carl is described as

> offen, ohne Verstellung, voll Feuer, lustig, zuweilen un-
> fleißig, machte seinen Eltern und seinen Lehrern durch
> manchen jugendlichen Streich Verdruß . . . Carl [erhielt]
> das Zeugnis eines leichtsinnigen, hupfenden Jünglings . . .
> Carls Temperament ward vom Strom ergriffen und zu man-
> chem Laster fortgerissen.[4]

This reflects Schiller's Karl only to a slight degree. The brother Wilhelm is described as serious and duty-conscious, much unlike Schiller's Franz.

II

The sources of most interest, at present, and of most significance for the understanding of the play, are all three of the works we have discussed: Goethes *Götz*, Lenz's *Hofmeister*, and Klinger's *Zwillinge* (possibly also his *Otto*, which contains an alienated son-figure Karl, much like Schiller's hero).[5] While many of the correspondences between *Die Räuber* and these sources could individually have been accidental (and some may be trivial), they gain significance in their entirety. In any case, the specific borrowed motifs are only the outward symbols of the same underlying problem of the split self. Against this thematic background they not only supply a coherence to Schiller's use of his sources, but also enable us to see how he assimilated and changed them in making them his own. Most importantly, they also help to establish an analysis of the play, based on the split self.

Götz is reflected, first of all, in the motif of the right hand. Schiller avoids an all too obvious reference to an iron hand by scattering various partial aspects of it through the play:

Franz. . . . Den Finger meiner rechten Hand wollte ich drum geben, dürft ich sagen, . . . (1.1.p.12)[6]

More distinctly, the henchman Hermann's fictitious account of Karl's death emphasizes the loss of the right hand: "Eine Kugel zerschmetterte ihm die rechte Hand, . . ." (2.2.-p.47).[7]

A (whole) hand is connected with iron: " . . . hubst du da nicht deine Hand zum eisernen Eid auf . . ." (5.2.p.132).[8]

The hand symbolizes, as in *Götz*, a binding of men: " . . . schwört mir das bey dieser männlichen Rechte. *Alle geben ihm die Hand*" (1.2.p.32).[9]

Finally, he treats the motif playfully: "Seht, hier bind ich meine rechte Hand an diesen Eichenast, ich bin ganz wehrlos, ein Kind kann mich umwerfen" (2.2.p.73).[10]

In another concrete borrowing Schiller even throws in a comet like that in *Götz* (2.2,p.52). More generally, Karl's *Kraftmensch* philosophy includes the same nostalgia for earlier ages and criticism of the weak contemporary society that was the message of *Götz:*

> Pfui! Pfui über das schlappe Kastraten-Jahrhundert, zu nichts nütze, als die Thaten der Vorzeit wiederzukäuen und die Helden des Alterthums mit Kommentationen zu schinden, und zu verhunzen mit Trauerspielen. (1.2.p.21)[11]

The reference to "tragedies" could be interpreted as Karl's desire to live what others can only fantasize about (a problem also expressed in Götz's son Karl, as we have seen), or as Schiller's self-ironic comment on his own undertaking in this work. The name of Karl's father, Maximilian, is the same as that of the Kaiser in *Götz.* The name of the play itself may have been derived from *Götz,* where the hero's enemies call him a "Räuber."

Some of this evidence, such as the comet or the name Maximilian, could easily be accidental, and the *Kraftmensch* philosophy became a stock sentiment of the times. Still, the careful treatment of the motif of the right hand implies that *Götz* was a conscious source for Schiller and increases the probability that the other similarities were consciously intended.

Lenz's *Hofmeister* is a likely source, in Pätus, for the figure of Spiegelberg. Both are radically emancipated; both attempt to win the central figure for their life style; and both are cowardly and dependent upon the stronger, more balanced personality. Moreover both are associated with the devil. Just as Pätus was chased by dogs, so Spiegelberg tells us how he sprang over a ditch to escape a vicious dog (1.2.p.23). The term "Hofmeister" or "hofmeistern" occurs three times in the work: (3.2.p.79; 3.2.p.83; and especially 4.5.p.109) where a rather enigmatic passage may not only refer to psychological influences on Karl's character, but may subtly reflect Lenz's play as well. There the alienation of the son results from a similar parental milieu:

> *Moor.* . . . eure fürchterlich klaffenden Wunden sind ja nur Glieder einer unzerbrechlichen Kette des Schicksals und

hängen zuletzt an meinen Feierabenden, an den Launen
meiner Ammen und Hofmeister, am Temperament meines
Vaters, am Blut meiner Mutter.[12]

Admittedly, this last speculation is largely a step into the
darkness; it is mentioned in the spirit of carrying out the
possible references to *Der Hofmeister* in a consequential way. A
"Hofmeister" is also mentioned in Schubart's story, but there
it has no apparent significance. Franz's assocation of Karl with
"Gassenjungen" (1.1.p.13), because of his early tendency to
run in the streets, together with the specific mention of
Leipzig in this connection, is reminiscent of Fritz, who also
runs off to Leipzig and who is described as "gassenläuferisch." More significantly, *Der Hofmeister* is a likely model for
Schiller's division of the self into three part selves: Franz,
Karl, and Spiegelberg.

The most important source for *Die Räuber* appears to have
been Klinger's *Die Zwillinge*, from which Schiller apparently
borrowed, to begin with, the figure of the evil son Guelfo (in
certain respects) for his Franz.[13] Franz uses the term "Zwillinge" (1.3.p.36) to describe his relationship to Karl, despite
the fact that they are not twins and have little or nothing in
common. He also represents, like Guelfo, the jealous, scheming, second-born son bent on inheriting the patriarchal wealth
and his brother's beloved. Where Klinger compares his
Guelfo and Grimaldi to Cassius and Brutus, Schiller introduces a song that plays upon the relationship between Brutus
as son and Caesar as father. It expresses in pure fashion the
father-son conflict that underlies the split-self problem:

Cesar. . . . Sohn—es war dein Vater—Sohn—die Erde/Wär
gefallen dir als Erbe zu./ Geh!—du bist der gröste Römer
worden,/ Da in Vaters Brust dein Eisen drang. . . . *Brutus.*
Vater, halt!—Im ganzen Sonnenreiche/ Habe ich Einen nur
gekannt,/ Der dem großen Cesar gleiche/ Diesen einen hast
du Sohn genannt. . . . Wo ein Brutus lebt muß Cesar ster-
ben,/ Geh du linkswärts, laß mich rechtswärts gehn. (4.5.p-
p.108–109)[14]

The person addressed in the last line, seemingly the father, might more meaningfully be seen as Franz as part of the whole son speaking through Brutus. In various places, (e.g., the positioning of the family portraits or the left scale in his dream) he is associated with the left, Karl with the right. If not, then the father's death, as opposed to the son's life, can hardly be explained as going to the left and the right, respectively.

Schiller also uses the name Amalia (Guelfo's mother) for Karl's beloved. Klinger (like Lenz in *Der Hofmeister*) mentions the motif of the Prodigal Son, as we have seen, and Schiller used this term ("Der verlorene Sohn") as an informal title for his play (letter of Nov. 3, 1781 to Dalberg).[15] The motif of tearing one's clothes down the middle, suggestive of tearing the self into two halves, occurs in *Die Zwillinge* (p.290) and in *Die Räuber* (4.5.p.114). Finally, the motif of the sword is treated similarly in both works, as will be noted below.[16]

From his own treatment of the split self, it is clear that Schiller must have grasped completely its significance in his sources. In his preface to the first edition and in his "Selbstrezension," he hints at this psychological level of the play. He alludes to a process of discovering "die Seele gleichsam bei ihren verstohlensten Operationen."[17]

Schiller felt this level to be too subtle to meet the eye of the casual theatergoer: "Die Kenner, die den Zusammenhang des Ganzen befassen, und die Absicht des Dichters erraten, machen immer das dünnste Häuflein aus."[18] In a letter to Reinwald, dated April 14, 1783, Schiller declared that

> in unserer Seele alle Karaktere nach ihren Urstoffen schlafen, und durch Wirklichkeit und Natur oder künstliche Täuschung ein daurendes oder nur illusorisch-und augenblikliches Daseyn gewinnen. Alle Geburten unsrer Phantasie wären also zuletzt nur *Wir selbst*.[19]

While this—like the corresponding comments of Herder and Lenz—is very general, it does directly support the identity of various main characters in *Die Räuber*. It also indicates a general conclusion that Schiller drew from his literary or psychological sources.

III

In the text the most direct and unambiguous suggestions of a unity of self hardly permit any other reading. As in *Die Zwillinge*, reference is frequently made to "the" son, where realistic language would require "that" or "this" or "a" son (of two) (1.1.,p.16; 2.2.,p.44;2.2.,p.50;4.5.p.114). As in *Der Hofmeister* and *Die Zwillinge*, Amalia pointedly refers to an *only* son:

> . . . schämt euch, ihr Unmenschen! schämt euch ihr Drachenseelen, ihr Schande der Menschheit!—seinen einzigen Sohn! *Franz*. Ich dächte, er hätt ihrer zween. (1.3.33)[20]

At the end of the play, Karl assumes that Amalia will not love him when she learns of his crimes as robber chieftain. He resists her embrace, only to be overwhelmed ("aufblühend") when she identifies and loves him as the whole son ("Einziger, unzertrennlicher!" (5.2.p.132), just as Ferdinando insisted on being accepted. In attempting to win over Amalia, Franz identifies himself with his brother in particularly unambiguous terms:

> . . . ich meynte immer, wir müßten Zwillinge seyn! und wär der leidige Unterschied von außen nicht, wobey leider freylich ich verlieren mus, wir würden zehnmal verwechselt. Du bist, sagt' ich oft zu mir selbst, ja du bist der ganze Karl, sein Echo, sein Ebenbild! (1.3.p.36)[21]

These direct motifs of unity take on content and definition first of all through two Biblical themes: Schiller—like Lenz and Klinger—alludes to the Prodigal Son (1.2.p.22) as a designation of emancipation and the desire ultimately to return to the father. To this source he adds his own Biblical borrowing from the story of Joseph, which reinforces the motif of emancipation and alienation. In 2.2 Amalia reads from the Bible the description of how the brothers bring the bloody cloth to Jacob as evidence of Joseph's death. Then Franz delivers to his father a bloody sword, with the same message about Karl. These Biblical sources do not imply a split self, but they do establish the underlying conflict between father and son. They also specifically illustrate the emancipation from the father and the rivalry with another son figure.

This basic Biblical theme of emancipation from the father eliminates possible confusion and misinterpretation of accents in clarifying the specific functions of Franz, Karl, and Spiegelberg as part-selves.[22] On this foundation their interrelationships can further be clarified by comparing them with their apparent literary sources. Spiegelberg's role is strikingly similar to that of Pätus, although in character he is more extreme in his quality as devil. Franz is still more closely linked to Guelfo, sharing both the role as scheming second son, jealous of his brother's inheritance and his beloved, and his evil character. But Guelfo's ideal was that of a *Kraftmensch* (like Leisewitz's Guido in *Julius von Tarent*), while Schiller reserves some of this quality for Karl and substitutes in Franz a more intellectual, Mephistophelian consequentiality.

Karl is somewhat more difficult to compare with literary models, if only because several sources—primarily Schubart, Lenz's Fritz, and the noble robber in *Don Quixote* (perhaps also Klinger's Karl in *Otto*)—may have overlapped in contributing to him. Like Schubart's Karl he was active and somewhat naughty as a boy and freely gave away money to beggars:

> *Franz.* Ahndete mir's nicht, da er noch ein Knabe den Mädels so nachschlenderte, mit Gassenjungen und elendem Gesindel auf Wiesen und Bergen sich herumhetzte, den Anblick der Kirche, wie ein Missethäter das Gefängnis, floh, und die Pfennige, die er Euch abquälte, dem ersten dem besten Bettler in den Hut warf. . . . (1.1.p.13)/[23]

Typical of the difficulties of pinning down the sources for Karl, this passage already points as much to the Prodigal Son and to Fritz as it does to Schubart's Carl. More specifically like Lenz's figure, however, Karl plays a role dominating over someone more radically emancipated than himself. In relation to these apparent sources for all three part-selves, Schiller has sharpened and exaggerated them. Each self is pushed to the logical extreme in whatever direction results from the basic elements of his character: Karl explores the bitter frontiers of exile, before even considering the obvious return home; Spiegelberg seems, as the devil, almost to lose human substance; and Franz is intoxicated with the possibilities of a total and consequential ruthlessness.

A closer look at these central figures shows how Schiller elaborated on this pattern of three part-selves. Spiegelberg's role is implied first of all in his name. He mirrors what is in Karl's soul. He reflects Karl's emancipation in its negative, literally devilish aspect (cf., for example, 1.2.p.30; 2.3). Thus Spiegelberg also directly shares motifs with Karl; for instance, when the priest, in an attempt to negotiate the robbers' surrender, compares Karl to Satan (2.3.p.68), or when he asks what devil speaks from his mouth (2.3.p.72). When Spiegelberg dies, Karl recognizes that his own end is approaching: "Ich verstehe—Lenker im Himmel—ich verstehe—die Zweige fallen vom Stamme—und mein Herbst ist kommen" . . . (4.5.p.107).[24]

It is Spiegelberg who conceives the plan for the robber band, and thus for Karl's way of life. As one who is totally emancipated, he is clever (1.2); but, like Pätus, he is weak and cowardly (1.2;4.5). His most peculiar utterance is explainable only from the point of view that as a more emancipated personality he sees Karl (as Pätus saw Fritz) as younger, tied to home and parents, hence childlike. When Karl returns home, Spiegelberg is enraged and plots to kill him, calling him an infant: "Komm! Zwey Pistolen fehlen selten, und dann—so sind wir die erste die den Säugling erdrosseln." (4.5.p.105).[25]

Outwardly this passage is incomprehensible, since on a realistic level Karl can hardly be considered an infant, even in exaggeration. But inwardly Karl's return home represents (from Spiegelberg's point of view) a regression to childhood.

The lack of connection between "pistols" and "strangle" makes no realistic sense either, unless the shift to the latter is recognized as a reference to Franz's death in that manner (pointing to the unity of Karl and Franz). Lest this peculiar motif go unnoticed, it appears also in the mouth of Schweizer: "Wenn ihm Leides geschehen wäre—Kameraden! wir zünden an und morden den Säugling" (4.5.p.104).[26]

Where Spiegelberg has Karl in mind, the loyal Schweizer can only mean Franz.[27] Thus Karl and Franz are subtly bound together here at a time when Karl, returning home, is encroaching upon Franz's psychological territory. Franz, unlike Karl, is ugly, and he suggests a unity with him when he identifies a sick, rotting man as his brother in order to horrify Amalia (1.3.pp.35–36). But Amalia escapes this threat. She *defines* Karl as not ugly while, incidentally, addressing Karl *in* Franz (unless the "du" is taken to shift suddenly from the distant beloved to Franz immediately after the address):

> Ha! Karl! Nun erkenn ich dich wieder! Du bist noch ganz! ganz! Alles war Lüge!—Weist du nicht, Bösewicht, daß Karl unmöglich das werden kann? *Franz steht einige Zeit tiefsinnig, dann dreht er sich plötzlich um zu gehen.* (1.3.p.36)[28]

Regretting his life as an outlaw, Karl later sees himself in terms of ugliness suggestive of Franz: "Und ich so heßlich auf dieser schönen Welt—und ich ein Ungeheuer auf dieser herrlichen Erde" (3.2.p.79).[29]

Supposing his father dead, Karl also temporarily assumes the guilt for Franz's deed:

> ...wo bin ich? Nacht vor meinen Augen—Schrecknisse Gottes—Ich, ich hab ihn getötet! *Er rennt davon.* (4.2.p.89)[30]

As the younger and home-bound self, Franz would be expected—if our hypothesis for the split self holds here—to be capable of love, while the later selves are not. In fact, Franz attempts to claim the inheritance of Karl's love for Amalia (1.2.p.37). When this fails, he threatens to take Amalia by force and insinuates his own image behind that of Karl:

> . . . das Schrekbild *Franz* soll hinter dem Bild deines Lieblings im Hinterhalt lauren, gleich dem verzauberten Hund, der auf unterirrdischen Goldkästen liegt. . . . (3.1.p.75)[31]

It may be significant that the imagery Franz uses here is in

Jungian terms suggestive of libido, both in respect to gold and to the significance of subterranean realms as reservoirs of energy in the unconscious. Karl, conversely, expressly renounces love when he forms the robber band (1.3.p.32).

Although he remains home and asserts a right to Amalia, Franz is not entirely what we would expect in the earliest of three temporal stages. In his cold intellectuality he resembles Spiegelberg. This raises the question whether we should see here a fundamentally temporal dimension of three selves or some sort of duality of character alone, more along the lines of *Die Zwillinge*, and supplemented by Spiegelberg as a reflection or projection of qualities found in Franz as well as in Karl. In his cynicism and desire for fame Spiegelberg resembles Franz (1.2); Buchwald (*op.cit.*, p.253) observes that Spiegelberg is a "caricature" of Franz. Otherwise Franz has no direct connection to Spiegelberg at all, while Karl is one of his closest companions. Thus Schiller apparently has attempted to use Spiegelberg both as a radically emancipated third stage (as in *Der Hofmeister*) and as a projection of, or mirror for, a dual self. It is understandable that even Schiller's synthetic genius could not assimilate both these dimensions with classic simplicity. He may in fact have been quite satisfied with a certain natural complexity obscuring the conceptual framework—much in the spirit of Lenz's procedure in *Der Hofmeister*. This is consistent with a remark in his preface to the first edition: " . . . drei außerordentliche Menschen zu erschöpfen, deren Tätigkeit von vielleicht tausend Räderchen abhänget, . . . "[32]

IV

Goethe expressed the ontogeny of the split self in *Götz* only indirectly in terms of the historical analogy, and left the psychological significance hidden in the personal, autobiographical background of the work. Nor was a more overt psychological treatment required there, since the historical perspective provided sufficient coherence. Lenz also did not depict any specific events creating the split, although he did adequately represent the unhealthy family constellation. Klinger also provided no explanation for the development of Guelfo's character, other than the question of the rights of the first-born, but let the Oedipal and incest theme supply the basis for alienation from the father and for a split between an infantile and a socialized self. Among these four, Schiller was the only one to provide a specific, traumatic incident that, by implication, marks or symbolizes the event of the split in the personality. Schiller himself drew attention to this aspect of the play. He showed his consciousness of the problem of the psychological development from childhood by asserting, in his *Selbstrezension,* that the dramatist had provided no explanation as to how a Franz could have developed:

> Unserem Jüngling, aufgewachsen im Kreis einer friedlichen schuldlosen Familie—woher kam ihm eine so herzverderbliche Philosophie? Der Dichter läßt uns diese Frage ganz unbeantwortet; . . . [33]

Yet in an abstract, symbolic manner the original split between Franz and Karl is subtly explained in the text—and why not, if Schiller the reviewer implied that such an explanation was needed? To be sure, the implications of the relevant passage account for Karl's emancipation, but not entirely for Franz's personality. When Karl returns home the old servant Daniel identifies him by a scar on his hand ("It was the right hand, too" [4.3.p.97]). Daniel then recounts the incident when the injury occurred:

> . . .da saßt ihr mir im Schoos, und rieft hotto! Und ich lief fort, Euch den Hottogaul zu holen—Jesus Gott! Warum mußt ich alter Esel auch fortlaufen?—Und wie mirs siedigheiß über den Rüken lief—wie ich das Zetergeschrei höre draußen im Oehrn, spring herein, und da lief das helle Blut, und laget am Boden, und hattet . . . Großer Gott, wenns ins Aug gegangen wäre. . . . Mein Lebenstag, sagt ich, soll mir kein Kind mehr ein Messer oder eine Schere oder so was spiziges, sagt ich, in die Hände kriegen, sagt ich,—war zum Glück noch Herr und Frau verreiset—
> . . . es heilte glüklich, bis auf die wüste Narbe. (4.3pp.96 –97) [34]

The symbolic weight of the passage is underscored by Daniel's failure to identify the sharp instrument, thus leaving it abstract. This incident unites three motifs central to the play—hand, sword, and scar—symbolizing a traumatic emancipation and accompanying wound. The hand signifies love, as in *Götz:*

> *Der alte Moor.* Oh ich fühl es tief was mir Amalia sagte, der Geist der Rache sprach aus ihrem Munde. Vergebens ausstreken deine sterbenden Hände wirst du nach einem Sohn, vergebens wähnen zu umfassen die warme Hand deines Karls . . . . (5.2.p.128)[35]

Logically, then, a wound to the hand, as in *Götz*, symbolizes a loss of love.

Peter Michelsen has argued that Schiller derived the sword motif, as well as a whole range of devices relating to gesture and pathos, specifically from Sacchini's *Calliroe,* which he attended in 1779, and that the function of the sword is to arouse the emotions of the spectator.[36] While Michelsen does not establish that Schiller understood such a function of the sword, he does uncover a plausible source for its use in *Die Räuber.* In any case, in the context of the split self, the sword (or lance) represents an emancipation that incorporates the sin of violence. The chief instrument of the robbers' crimes, the sword separates Karl from Amalia when a robber steps between them and reminds Karl of his oath (5.2.p.132). The robbers claim, in effect, that Karl cannot undo what he has done, cannot simply return to a love he has inwardly renounced. In the face of Amalia's love Karl's sword sinks, but only momentarily. (5.2.p.129). In its emancipatory function the sword has become a symbol of death and the only goal for the one who has chosen this path:

> *Amalia singt und spielt auf der Laute.* Willst dich Hektor ewig mir entreißen,/Wo des Aeaciden mordend Eisen/ Dem Patroklus schröklich Opfer bringt?/ Wer wird künftig deinen Kleinen lehren,/ Speere werfen und die Götter ehren,/ wenn hinunter dich der Xanthus schlingt?*Moor nimmt die*

Laute stillschweigend und spielt: Theures Weib, geh, hol die Todeslanze—/ Laß—mich fort—zum wilden Kriegestanze—(4.4.p.103)[37]

The same basic meaning of the sword is found in *Die Zwillinge:* "Blutig schwingt der Todesengel das würgende Schwert" (*op.cit.*, p.286).[38]

The underlying function of the sword as a symbol of the psychological act of alienation is also found in Klinger's play: "Ich ziehe mein Schwert und beginne den Schwur" (p.255).[39]

As a reflection of his childhood trauma, Hermann's presentation of a bloody sword, along with a fictitious story of Karl's death, not only extends the parallel to Joseph, as noted, but helps to unite the Biblical story with the act of emancipation and renunciation of love that creates the split self.

The motif of the scar serves as a tie, a physical reminder of the fateful incident of emancipation, and suggests a quality of defect, of violence done to nature. The scar is associated with the exploits of the robbers, binding them in loyalty to one another and to their way of life: "*Die Räuber durcheinander, reißen ihre Kleider auf:* Schau her, schau! Kennst du diese Narben? Du bist unser!"(5.2.p.132)[40]

Thus after Karl, accepting the moral imperative of this fate, has killed Amalia with his sword, he remembers these words: "*Mit bitterem Gelächter.* Die Narben, die böhmischen Wälder! Ja ja! Das muste freylich bezahlt werden (5.2.p.134)."[41]

As something less than a human being, Spiegelberg cannot acquire a scar: "*Schweizer.* Die Bestie ist dem Hauptmann immer giftig gewesen, und hat keine Narbe auf ihrer ganzen Haut . . . "(4.5.p.106).[42]

This helps to explain the somewhat scurrilous comment that Spiegelberg was born circumcised: "Ich bin freylich wunderbarerweiss schon voraus beschnitten" (1.2.p.22).[43]

In a substantial essay on the figure of Spiegelberg, Phillip F. Veit has marshaled evidence for his Jewishness, specifically as a reflection of Messianic sects who sought to create a new society. This can be viewed, in the present context, as a negative extreme of Karl's rebellion against a social order.

Veit derives Spiegelberg's claim of having been circumcised "in advance" from a "Midrashic myth according to which the Messiah was to be prenatally circumcised, a distinction he shares with other celebrated figures in Jewish mythology."[44]

Veit's argument points to an additional dimension in Spiegelberg. Unless the motifs of the scar and the wound are accidental—a possibility that the interlocking evidence of the motifs rules out—we have here a good example of Schiller's synthetic gift in intertwining the two themes of psychological emancipation and Messianic social revolution. If the motif of Spiegelberg's circumcision is derived from the Jewish tradition, then its actual function in the play must be seen to shift more to the personal level of the split self, since Spiegelberg cannot be seen as a Messiah; nor can Schiller be accused of a vicious anti-Semitic travesty.

V

Unlike Klinger and Lenz, Schiller had no direct personal connection with Goethe for his discovery of the split self. *Die Räuber* was the fruit of his intelligence as a reader. In many ways his play summarizes and culminates this central line of Storm and Stress plays; hence, in large measure, the Storm and Stress movement itself. Each of the four dramatists developed the theme in a manner expressive of his own concerns. Despite Schiller's emphasis on a synthesis of sources, this personal dimension is no less prominent here than in any of the predecessors. His own stubborn moral dialectic emerges here in contrast to Goethe's concern with the loss of his childhood environment and personality; Lenz's almost masochistic self-abnegation; and Klinger's Oedipus-tinged *Kraftmensch*.

This peculiarly Schillerian moral stubbornness, while inherent in the entire play, interjects itself decisively into the plot at the end. In the process of reintegrating the self Karl discovers, after returning home, what Franz has done to his father. Rather than accept the full burden for this crime he renounces any unity of self: " . . . das Band der Natur ist entzwey, die alte Zwietracht ist los, der Sohn hat seinen Vater erschlagen" (4.5.p.114).[45]

Karl is torn between the desire to regain love (and, more broadly speaking, a divine gift of life itself) and the compulsion to dissociate himself from Franz's crimes. The ultimate decision comes here, at the end, and passes by easily unnoticed in the rapid pace of the work. Amalia has given Karl the chance to return to her as the whole son, including the Franz personality ("Einziger, unzertrennlicher!" [5.2.p.132]). But Karl's momentary ecstasy is immediately extinguished by the robbers' claims upon him. To accept Amalia's love now would be to reintegrate the self and to take responsibility for all of Franz's monstrousness. Karl must choose between a larger, natural (if extreme) compass of human qualities and his moral integrity. He elects the latter, still salvageable with a noble surrender.[46]

We can imagine the editor of *Werther* arising from that doomed soul before its extinction, allowing Goethe to continue both cleansed and bereft of this youthful passion. So, also, we may imagine Schiller as having expressed in *Die Räuber* a choice of personality sacrificing a childhood vitality to moral and intellectual values. Perhaps significantly, Schiller's writing of *Die Räuber* can be seen as bringing about the emancipation from the *Karlsschule* as well as the forced exile from his native Württemberg and his parents (resulting from the conflict with Duke Karl Eugen, who had ordered him, as cadet in his elite military school, to cease his activity as a dramatist) that appear to be expressed in the work. Similarly, the problem of engagement treated in "Das Urteil" anticipated corresponding events in Kafka's life. In any case the turmoil of Schiller's sudden emancipation, exile, and infatuation with his landlady, Luise Vischer—all leavened by his sudden success as a dramatist—led Emil Ermatinger to a description of this period especially appropriate to our discussion:

Schillers Wesen, von Natur gespalten, bricht in einer geradezu furchtbaren Weise auseinander. Sinne und Geist gehen völlig getrennte Wege. . . . Aber diese idealische

Ueberstiegenheit war nur die eine Seite von Schillers
Geist. Die andere wühlte mit einer wilden Wollust im
Schmutze niedriger Sinnlichkeit.[47]

Like Klinger, Schiller recapitulated the split self theme (in
echoes) in a late work : *Die Braut von Messina* (1803). Despite
its sophisticated accompanying theory (Ueber den Gebrauch
des Chors in der Tragödie)—or perhaps because of this
emphasis—the play regresses in character development to the
baroque atmosphere of *Die Zwillinge* or *Julius von Tarent*. No
longer a central, vital concern to Schiller, the split self is not
manifest in the narrow sense of an underlying, original unity
of two brothers as part-selves. Instead he emphasizes the idea
of forging a new unity of the brothers, inimical to one another
since birth. The key to such unification is love. The mother
Isabella expresses the incongruence of their enmity and her
single love:

Vergessen ganz musst ich den *einen* Sohn,/Wenn ich der
Nähe mich des andern freute./ O meine Mutterliebe ist nur
eine,/ Und meine Söhne waren ewig zwei![48]

Unknown to one another, both brothers fall in love with the
same girl. Both are mysteriously attracted by a feeling of inner
unity which, they discover, results from her being their sister.
The younger *Kraftmensch* Don Cesar finds Don Manuel in her
arms and kills him. Learning only afterwards of her identity,
he executes himself, expecting to achieve in death a unification with his dead brother:

Doch ich, der Mörder, sollte glücklich sein,/ Und deine
heil'ge Unschuld ungerächet/ Im tiefen Grabe liegen—Das
verhüte/Der allgerechte Lenker unsrer Tage,/Daß solche
Teilung sei in seiner Welt—(last scene, p.94)[49]

It is interesting to note that Schiller does not permit the
violent Don Cesar to drop into the pure amorality of a Franz,
Guido, or Guelfo. Instead, Don Cesar reunites the self—or
rather himself and his brother—in death. To the extent that
Don Cesar resembles Franz and Don Manuel Karl, *Die Braut*

von Messina reverses and perhaps attempts to undo the result of *Die Räuber.* In the earlier work, Karl's return caused the extinction of the unsocialized *Kraftmensch.* Here the latter type destroys the older, more positive moral personality. Once he has done so and recognized his error, Don Cesar seems to change, to speak for the debt owed his brother; hence, to some degree, he functions for both. But this theme is not developed in any depth. By itself, moreover, *Die Braut von Messina* focuses not on a single, fragmented personality so much as on a larger principle of human relatedness. Although this is demonstrated here in a family, it suggests a universal level of mankind unified in love.

Notes

1. "Is this drama a straggler from the Storm and Stress, does it belong in the same line as the drama of a Lenz, Klinger, Leisewitz, as that of the young Goethe . . . ? Or must one view *Die Räuber* in connection with the tradition of the European Enlightenment, with the purpose of 'bringing down vice and avenging religion, morals and bourgeois laws upon their enemies'? . . . Until today the criticism has not been able to answer such questions unambiguously. To be sure, in evaluation it has often allied itself with the negative judgments of the nineteenth century in denying the young poet any psychological talent and finding his characters intolerably extreme and distorted." (Benno von Wiese, *Friedrich Schiller* [Stuttgart: Metzler, 1963], pp.136–137).

2. Gerhart Storz, *Der Dichter Friedrich Schiller* (Stuttgart: Ernst Klett, 1959), p.25.

3. Fritz Martini, "Die feindlichen Brüder. Zum Problem des gesellschaftskritischen Dramas von J. A. Leisewitz, F. M. Klinger and F. Schiller," *Jahrbuch der deutschen Schillergesellschaft* 16 (1972): 208–65.

4. " . . . open, without deceit, full of fire, cheerful, sometimes lazy, irritated his parents and teachers with youthful pranks . . . Carl was regarded as a carefree, playful boy . . . Carl's temperament was seized by the current and swept away to many a vice." (Christian Daniel Schubart, *Schubarts Werke in einem Band,* ed. Ursula Wertheim and Hans Böhm [Weimar: Volksverlag, 1959], p.742).

5. Alfred Keller has compared *Die Räuber* at length with *Otto (Die literarischen Beziehungen zwischen den Erstlingsdramen Klingers und Schillers* [Ph.D. diss., Bern, 1911]). While Keller concludes that *Otto* was a primary source for Schiller, his evidence suggests more a general, diffuse relationship; indicating Schiller's thirst for the raw material he needed to compensate for his relative lack of life experience. Keller also notes a number of brother conflicts in *Otto,* but these comparisons also lack focus and depth (pp.21–22,37–41).

6. "*Franz.* . . . I'd give the finger of my right hand for it, if I could say . . . " (Johann Christoph Friedrich Schiller, *Schillers Werke* [Nationalausgabe], vol. 3: *Die Räuber,* ed. Herbert Stubenrauch [Weimar: H. Böhlaus Nachfolger, 1953]). Quotations are from the "Schauspiel" edition of Tobias Löffler, 1782.

7. "A ball shattered his right hand."

8. "Didn't you raise your hand to an iron oath . . . "

9. "Swear by this manly right hand." *(All give him their hands.)*

10. "Look, here I'm tying my right hand to this oak branch, I'm entirely helpless, a child can knock me over."

11. "To the devil with the flabby century of eunuchs, good for nothing but chewing over the deeds of antiquity and flaying the ancient heroes with commentaries and disfiguring them with tragedies."

12. "Your horrid, gaping wounds are only links in an unbreakable chain of fate and depend ultimately on my leisure time, the moods of my nurses and tutors, the temperament of my father, the blood of my mother."

13. That Schiller was influenced by Klinger (leaving aside the question of which of Klinger's works) is well established in the Schiller literature. Schiller made the point himself in a letter to Wilhelm von Wolzogen dated Sept. 4, 1803: "Sage dem General Klinger, wie sehr ich ihn schätze. Er gehört zu denen, welche vor 25 Jahren zuerst und mit Kraft auf meinen Geist gewirkt haben." (Fritz Jonas, *Schillers Briefe*) 7 vols. [Stuttgart, Berlin, Leipzig: Deutsche Verlagsanstalt, 1892–96], 7:70). John G. Robertson (*Schiller After a Century* [Edinburg and London: William Blackwood and Sons, 1905]) identified especially *Die Zwillinge* as an immediate source for *Die Räuber* (along with Leisewitz's *Julius von Tarent* and Schubart's "Zur Geschichte des menschlichen Herzens"), but gave no particulars (p.29). More generally, Robertson recognized in Schiller's play "one of those intuitive works of genius which appear sporadically in a nation's history, and gather together all the threads o[f] vital interest peculiar to an age" (p.27).

14. *Caesar.* . . . Son—it was your father—son—the earth/Would have fallen to you as your heritage./Go!—you have become the greatest Roman,/Since your iron plunged in your father's breast . . . *Brutus.* Father, stop!—In the whole realm of the sun/I have only known One/Who equals the great Caesar/This one you called son . . . . where a Brutus lives Caesar must die,/Go to the left, let me go to the right."

15. Bodo Lecke, ed., *Friedrich Schiller. Von den Anfängen bis 1795* (Dichter über ihre Dichtungen; Munich: Heimeran, 1969), p.100. But Stubenrauch believes that this title, only temporarily considered, was Dalberg's idea (*op.cit.*, pp. 313–15).

16. For two other specific borrowings from *Die Zwillinge* see Stubenrauch, *op.cit*, pp.404,408. In addition to these concrete motifs, a certain influence of Klinger on Schiller's language is likely, specifically passages characterized by explosive repetitions of individual words (see especially 4.3,p.99). Else Münch compared these two works ("Schillers *Räuber* und Klingers *Zwillinge*," *Zeitschrift für Deutschkunde* 10 [1932]: 710–21), focussing on the style. But she saw more a quality of "Predigtstil," "die Sprache der Bibel" in Schiller's play as a contrast to Klinger's explosiveness (p.717).

17. " . . . the soul as it were in its most secret operations." Storz has attempted to account for Schiller's claim of psychological depth in a different manner. Discounting any psychological realism on the part of the young poet, he concludes that the real psychology here consists of a kind of religious grandiosity (both in good and evil) of the characters (*op.cit.*, p.50). R. Masson has accounted for Schiller's claim of psychological realism in terms of his psychological studies at the *Karlsschule*, and applied them to Franz's poorly motivated suicide. ("Un ancêtre de Franz Moor," *Etudes Germaniques* 25(1) [1970]: 1-6). But the reasons for Franz's suicide represent only a small part of the difficult motivational problems of the play, most of which probably cannot be solved without simply relegating the external action to a secondary issue.

18. "The experts who grasp the unity of the whole are only a tiny group" (Lecke, p.8).

19. "In our soul all characters sleep in the form of their basic meanings and through reality and nature or artificial illusion win a lasting or only illusory and momentary existence. All offspring of our fantasy thus are in the last analysis only *we ourselves*" (Ibid. For a discussion of this see the study by Gisa Heyn, *Der junge Schiller als Psychologe* [Zürich: Juris Verlag, 1966], p.71).

20. "Shame on you, you monsters! Shame on you, you dragon souls, you dregs of humanity—his only son! *Franz.* I thought he had two of them."

21. "I always thought we had to be twins! And if it weren't for the sole difference on the outside, whereby admittedly I must lose, we would be mistaken for one another ten times over. You are, I often said to myself, yes you are the whole Karl, his echo, his image!" Stubenrauch found the deletion of this passage by an editor of one version of the play entirely laudable: "Denn die Behauptung innerster Seelenverwandtschaft überschreitet auch als blanke Heuchelei die Grenze des Zumutbaren" (*op.cit.*, p.406).

22. Cf. the insight of Benno von Wiese, *op.cit.*, p.145: "Beide Brüder vergegenwärtigen ein gestörtes Vehältnis zur Familie und vor allem zu dem autoritären Pol der Familie: zum Vater. Nicht der Konflikt der Brüder ist das dramatische Thema, sondern die gestörte Vaterordnung."

23. "*Franz.* That's what I always thought, when as a boy he chased the girls around, ran about the mountains and meadows with street urchins and miserable trash, fled the sight of church as a miscreant flees prison, and threw the pennies he harassed from you into the hat of the first beggar to come along."

24. "*Moor thinking.* I understand—guiding hand in heaven—I understand—the branches fall from the trunk—and my autumn has come."

25. "Come! Two pistols are seldom hard to find, and then—we'll be the first to strangle the infant."

26. "If something happened to him—Comrades! We burn, and murder the infant."

27. In his textual notes to *Die Räuber* (*op.cit.*, p.428), Stubenrauch comments that the sense of this passage is "morden *selbst* den Säugling," assuming that Karl cannot possibly be meant. But this suggestion lacks all text-critical justification, as Stubenrauch's own extraordinarily thorough scholarship shows.

28. "Ha! Karl! Now I recognize you again! You are still whole! whole! It was all a lie!—Don't you know, rascal, that Karl cannot possibly turn into that? *Franz stands for a time deep in thought, then turns suddenly around to go.*"

29. "And I so ugly on this beautiful earth—and I a monster on this splendid planet."

30. "Where am I? Night in front of my eyes—Terrors of God—I, I killed him!" *(He runs away.)*

31. "The fearful image of *Franz* will lie in ambush behind the image of your dear one, like the spellbound dog that lies on subterranean chests of gold."

32. " . . . to exhaust three extraordinary people whose activity is determined by perhaps a thousand little wheels." (Lecke, p.109.)

33. "Our youthful hero, grown up in the circle of a peaceful guiltless family—where did he come by such a ruinous philosophy? The poet leaves this question totally unanswered." (Ibid., p.121.)

34. " . . . you sat on my lap and called 'horsie!' and I ran off to get you the hobby horse—Jesus Lord! Why did this old ass have to run off?—and how it ran boiling hot over my back—how I hear the scream outside in the vestibule, rush in, and there the bright blood ran, and you lay on the floor and had . . . Lord, if it had gone into your

eye . . . The rest of my days, I said, no child will ever again get his hands on a knife or a scissors or something sharp like that—fortunately the master and mistress were away . . . it healed well except for the ugly scar."

35. "*The elder Moor.* O I feel deeply what Amalia said to me, the spirit of revenge spoke from her mouth. In vain will you stretch out your dying hands for a son, in vain think you are grasping the warm hand of your Karl. . . .

36. Peter Michelsen, "Studien zu Schillers *Räubern,*" *Jahrbuch der deutschen Schillergesellschaft* 8(1964):57 – 111, pp.60 – 61.

37. "*Amalia sings and plays on the lute.* Would you, Hector, forever tear yourself from me,/Where Achilles' murderous iron/Brings fearful sacrifice to Patroklus?/Who will teach your little ones/To throw spears and honor the gods,/When the Xanthus has swallowed you?/*Moor takes the lute silently and plays.* Worthy woman, go, fetch the lance of death—/Let me go to the wild dance of war."

38. "Bloody swings the angel of death the murderous sword."

39. "I draw my sword and begin the oath."

40. "*The robbers tear open their clothes.* Look here, look! Do you know these scars? You belong to us!"

41. "*With bitter laughter.* The scars, the Bohemian forests! Yes, yes! That had to be paid for."

42. "*Schweizer.* The beast has always hated the captain and has no scar on his whole skin."

43. "Miraculously, I was circumcised in advance."

44. Philipp F. Veit, "The Strange Case of Moritz Spiegelberg," *Germanic Review* 44 (1969): 171 – 85, p.181.

45. "The ties of nature are broken, the old division is alive ʳhe son has slain his father."

46. Ilse Graham has discussed *Die Räuber* against a similar backdrop of the problem of an integrated human personality. While she does not recognize in Franz and Karl parts of a whole self, she does see clearly Karl's incompleteness and grasps Schiller's deep concern for this problem. Interestingly, she sees this one-sidedness of Karl's choice of personality avenging itself and working itself out in the course of the play, somewhat in contrast to our perception of Karl's final choice at the end. (*Schiller's Drama: Talent and Integrity* [London: Methuen, 1974], pp.93 – 109).

47. "Schiller's personality, by nature dualistic, breaks apart in a fearful fashion. Mind and desires go completely separate ways . . . But this idealistic excess was only the one side of Schiller's mentality. The other rolled with a wild pleasure in the mud of low sensuality." (Emil Ermatinger, *Deutsche Dichter 1700 – 1900. Zweiter Teil.* [Bonn: Athenäum Verlag, 1949], pp.45,46).

48. "I had to completely forget the *one* son,/If I enjoyed the company of the other./O my mother-love is only *one,*/And my sons were always two!" (*Die Braut von Messina,* vol. 2 of *Friedrich Schiller. Sämtliche Werke,* ed. Gerhard Fricke and Herbert G. Göpfert [Munich: Carl Hanser, 1959], p.834).

49. "But I, the murderer, should be happy,? And let your holy innocence lie unavenged/In the bottom of the grave—that forbid/The just guide of our days,/That such division should exist in his world—"

Part II

The poets discussed in Part 2 are less focused in time than those in Part 1. They also lack the personal unification that went out from Goethe. Indeed, between Grillparzer and Wedekind lies a considerable gulf of intellectual history. On one side we find a poet whose stylistic instincts drew him back to Goethe and Schiller and even to the baroque, and whose poetic medium constantly flirted with a Mozartean elegance, a musicality suggestive of the opera. On the other side is Wedekind, a pioneer of the twentieth century, caustically prosaic, more an outcast and destroyer of his time than the harbored child that Grillparzer came to be, albeit belatedly, in his. In the works of Kafka we experience a nightmarish world that is bedded upon a disillusioning analysis and a consciousness diametrically opposed to the soft flow of Grillparzer's fairy-tale realm. But Kafka at least manages to remain psychically immersed in the reality of his poetic world. Broch, finally, assumes an ever increasing conscious responsibility for his, until the entire structure stylistically disintegrates in the fragmentation of the narrative perspective into isolated plot-lines and modes of narration in the third novel of *Die Schlaf-wandler*.

While more closely related to the eighteenth century than the twentieth, stylistically speaking, Grillparzer's "Der arme Spielmann" and *Die Jüdin von Toledo* influenced or anticipated to a significant degree the other poets of this section in thematic terms. A direct influence reaches from Grillparzer to Kafka and through Kafka to Broch, whereas Wedekind (and, through him, Hasenclever) drew his recognition of the split self from Goethe. But in more general terms of psychosexual self-analysis Grillparzer anticipated a modern preoccupation characteristic of all the poets discussed in Part 2.

The fact remains, however, that the split-self theme as discussed in Part 1 reflects a concentrated, unified poetic and psychological innovation, while its presence in Part 2 has more the character of diffuse, partly random echoes of Goethe. If every intellectual movement launches its most essential and vital concerns into perpetuity, then perhaps the poets of Part 2 realized and demonstrated part of the lasting heritage of the *Geniezeit*.

The new science of psychology, in contrast, influenced the tradition of the split self only gradually and tangentially. Where Wedekind and Hasenclever did not yet perceive this new field as a major source of inspiration, Kafka experimented only uncertainly and ambivalently with its concepts. Psychology as a science served these writers at best to raise to full conscious understanding psychological material already borne adequately by literary sources. Examples of this may be seen in Kafka's treatment of masochism (in "Die Verwandlung" and "Ein Hungerkünstler"), a theme he perceived in Sacher-Masoch's *Venus im Pelz;* perhaps also in Grillparzer's "Armer Spielmann." Only Broch, among the writers discussed here, raised psychology (Freud and Jung) to a source of thematic material on an equal basis with literary models.

The split-self theme, then, as realized by the authors of this section, does not result from the coming of age of modern psychology, but from a broader intellectual awakening that began in the eighteenth century.

5

Franz Grillparzer: "Der Arme Spielmann" and *Die Jüdin von Toledo*

I

The split self has been widely acknowledged in Grillparzer's short story, "Der arme Spielmann." The work has also been interpreted in unusual detail, particularly in the analyses of Richard Brinkmann and Heinz Politzer.[1] John M. Ellis has drawn together the numerous scattered critical references to the split self.[2] But Ellis believes that these lead into a fruitless biographism, and he prefers to dwell on the theme of "integrity in relation to efficiency" (p.134). This wariness of the biographical is justified only to the extent that the literature has not attempted to explore the identity of the narrator and the Spielmann, except to note that they both reflect aspects of Grillparzer. Günther Jungbluth, for example, has analyzed the correspondences between Grillparzer and the two main figures of the story. He concludes that it represents not only a "merciless judgment" of Grillparzer upon himself, but also—in connection with a diary comment—"a document of extreme self-pleasure."[3]

Of more immediate interest, at present, is the study of Eleonore Frey-Staiger: *Grillparzer: Gestalt und Gestaltung des Traums*.[4] She has treated the question of a *Spaltung* of Grillparzer in his work into the "play" and "spectator" (p.89), or inward and outward relationships to reality. She has followed this perspective into related issues, and her approach gains much from its broad application to Grillparzer's work as a whole. To be sure, she has little to say about "Der arme Spielmann," where Jakob is a good example of the inward self (pp. 115–16), and where the narrator can be understood in terms of an outward self (although she does not mention him). Beyond this, what the narrator and the Spielmann represent and the sense of their interaction have not been examined closely in the context of their function as part-selves. This will be our point of departure.

The relationship between the narrator and the Spielmann fits into the pattern we have designated as a norm for our theme. On the one hand is the Spielmann, with his childhood story of paternal oppression and his unrequited love for Barbara, a girl from the lower class. These two problems precisely match the characteristics of the oppressed earlier self. His counterpart is the narrator, intellectually and emotionally emancipated to the point where his polished exterior becomes suspect. Only an explicit inability to love cannot be directly confirmed in the text as an attribute of this personality. Since we learn almost nothing beyond what he reveals in his narration, his own part-self characteristics must remain largely masked; therefore, we cannot speak of a directly developed theme of his inability to love. Nevertheless, two telling details emerge in his narration: his condescending (or perhaps self-protective) distance from the Spielmann and the absence of any mention of his own social or family environment. We learn merely that when he is not engaged in the new hobby of following the Spielmann, his activities tend to vacillate between "thoughtless diversion" and "self-torturing melancholy."[5] Thus in following the Spielmann he betrays at least a lack of, and a need for, human involvement. Indeed, as the object of his curiosity implicitly suggests, he is the "beneficiary" ("der Beschenkte," p. 152) in their relationship.

While these facts in themselves are insufficient to establish the characteristics of the emancipated type, they gain definition against the broader backdrop of Christianity. Although this lightly but precisely developed theme is not immediate to the narrator's character, it is emphatic in its universality. The Christian symbolism begins with the narrator's attendance at the Brigittenau festival as "a pilgrimage, a religious devotion" (p.148). Later the Spielmann—goal of this pilgrimage—is described as feeling "his own wounds and those of others" (p.160), a combination pointing uniquely to Christ. At the end his violin, placed next to a mirror, is juxtaposed to a crucifix. If the violin represents the Spielmann and the crucifix Christ, then the mirror (in its proximity to the violin) can be seen to connect, through the content of its reflection, either Spielmann and Christ or Spielmann and the viewer; i.e., the narrator. If Christ represents above all the principle of love, then we find here a universal backdrop for the vague "freeing of pleasure" ("Losgebundenheit der Lust") associated with the narrator's "pilgrimage" (p.146). Through this Christian symbolism the festival thus expresses the narrator's need and search for—and hence presumably his relative lack of—love. The Christ symbolism is also directly tied to the split-self theme: "Teile des Ganzen, . . . in dem denn doch zuletzt das Göttliche liegt"(p.148).[6]

Each of these examples appears to serve a specific purpose: the Christ principle is established within the Spielmann; the search for Christ is revealed in the narrator; and the God-principle consists of the unity, if not necessarily of narrator and Spielmann, then at the very least of the social classes each represents. The Christ theme functions here not as a thick gratuitous layer of religious allegory to substitute for any lack of independent substance, but as an element carefully and minimally infused into the text. It is meant to suggest the universality of the Spielmann's condition, the narrator's possibly unconscious search for love, and the unity of the two. The evidence does not suggest a crude equation of the Spielmann and Christ.

Thus the constellation of the four basic characteristics of the split-self theme (oppression and love versus emancipation and inability to love) dominates the text. That Grillparzer also intended the narrator and the Spielmann specifically as parts of a single whole self is clear not only from his obvious relationship to them (as has been noted widely in the secondary literature), but explicitly from the text itself. At the beginning the narrator's description of the festival contains references that are less significant for their superficial function to describe a social phenomenon than for their applicability to the narrator and the Spielmann—the prime representatives here of the two social classes:

> In Wien ist der Sonntag nach dem Vollmonde im Monat Juli jedes Jahres samt dem darauf folgenden Tage ein eigentliches Volksfest, wenn je ein Fest diesen Namen verdient hat. Das Volk besucht es und gibt es selbst; und wenn Vornehmere dabei erscheinen, so können sie es nur in ihrer Eigenschaft als Glieder des Volks. Da ist keine Möglichkeit der Absonderung; . . . (P.146)[7]

More emphatically, this event unites parts of a whole:

> . . . als ein Liebhaber der Menschen, sage ich, besonders wenn sie in Massen für einige Zeit der einzelnen Zwecke vergessen und sich als Teile des Ganzen fühlen, in dem denn doch zuletzt das Göttliche liegt—. . . (P.148)[8]

The narrator continues, explicitly shifting the sense from the societal to the personal: " . . . als einem solchen ist mir jedes Volksfest ein eigentliches Seelenfest, eine Wallfahrt, eine Andacht" (p.148).[9]

The psychological significance of this for the narrator is, to begin with, a "burst of joy, the freeing of pleasure" (p.146); that is, if we may ascribe to the narrator the same basic motives he attributes to the visitors to the festival in general. All of this takes place in an atmosphere that a "new arrival" might find "dubious" ("bedenklich," p.146). Leaving aside for the moment the question of where this problem may lead, we find in the Spielmann a corresponding yearning for unity, as expressed in his violin playing:

> . . . und so bearbeitete er eine alte vielzersprungene Violine, wobei er den Takt nicht nur durch Aufheben und Niedersetzen des Fußes, sondern zugleich durch übereinstimmende Bewegung des ganzen gebückten Körpers markierte. Aber all the Bemühung Einheit in seine Leistung zu bringen, war fruchtlos. (p.149;[10]

"Unity" is not entirely the expected expression for the superficial sense of this passage. One would ordinarily expect something like "order," "accuracy," "intonation" or "proper rhythm." Unity here is better understood in connection with the unity that the narrator, as a counterpart to the Spielmann, seeks in the festival. If this is the case, then both narrator and Spielmann lack—and seek—unity.

This much would establish the story within the bounds of our narrowly defined split-self problem as a consciously manipulated theme. In contrast to most of his predecessors, however, Grillparzer seems to have benefited neither from the advice of a Herder nor from the confidences of a Goethe in gaining insight into this problem. Like Schiller, he may have perceived the theme in earlier works. If so—unlike Schiller—he gave no indication of having done so, either in the text or in his other writings. While he had used *Die Räuber* as a model for *Die Ahnfrau,* as Wolfgang Paulsen has demonstrated, it may be significant that he borrowed only one son figure (Karl, in Jaromir) and included no hint of a split self in this play. Similarly, while we know that he read *Götz von Berlichingen* in his youth, no other textual or biographical evidence points to Goethe as a source for his use of the split self.[11] In short, any of the works already discussed could have influenced him, but no concrete evidence appears to be forthcoming.

II

Having established substantial evidence of the split self here, we should consider some additional questions closely related to the theme. An important stylistic motif, often reiterated, points to the fairy tale, or perhaps the art fairy tale of the *Romantik.*[12] The superficial realism of the story is, above all, belied by the extreme relationship of the Spielmann to his father. With a violent gesture the latter rejects his son's attempt to kiss his hand and then condemns him prophetically: "Ce gueux" (p. 160). When the Spielmann is seen in Barbara's shop, he is presumably recognized as consorting with the lower classes, although realistically this cannot be all that much of a crime. Nevertheless, he is banished, Cinderella-like, to an isolated room, as though imprisoned. This scene points forward, to be sure, to Kafka, but also backward to the childlike exaggerations and stylisations of the fairy tale. Specific motifs suggest Eichendorff's "Aus dem Leben eines Taugenichts": the infinite guilelessness of the Spielmann, totally ignorant of society and oblivious to events he should be directing (the arrangements for his father's funeral and the disposition of the estate); the mysterious "secret warner" (p.172); the simple satisfaction that, despite all adversity, he has "God's grace"; and the fairy-tale syntax:

> Ich fiel auf die Knie und betete laut und konnte nicht begreifen, daß ich das holde Gotteswesen einmal gering geschätzt, ja gehaßt in meiner Kindheit und küßte die Violine und drückte sie an mein Herz und spielte wieder und fort. (P. 162)[13]

Such tones bring Grillparzer's text close to a Jungian perspective on the fairy tale as manifesting archetypes of the unconscious. The simplemindedness and purity of the Spielmann suggest the Jungian analysis of the fairy-tale archetype of the disadvantaged child who is bullied by two siblings and a single parent of the same sex.[14] Frequently seen as simple or even mentally retarded, this figure represents the undeveloped unconscious—outwardly helpless but possessing great potential ("God's grace"). Thus the Spielmann appears as black sheep among three brothers and is oppressed by his father, with no mention of a mother. The two brothers are then replaced by the two "trade apprentices"—a suggestion that Grillparzer recognized or intuited the importance of maintaining this pattern.

Grillparzer may not in fact have had any inkling of such a level of significance. He may have used such fairy-tale material merely as a useful idiom to express the simplicity of the Spielmann and his harsh treatment at the hands of others. Still, this level—intentionally or not—perfectly corresponds to the Spielmann's role as the childhood part of the split self. The child is unsocialized and has not yet learned to repress completely those aspects of the psyche that form the unconscious. This pattern is also commensurate with his capacity for love and with the narrator as the juxtaposed adult, conscious ego, socialized to the point of pompous sophistication. The idea of a second self, repressed within or behind the public personality, may indeed constitute an inner meaning for what ostensibly refers to the universality of human characteristics: " . . . und wahrlich! man kann die Berühmten nicht verstehen, wenn man die Obskuren nicht durchgefühlt hat" (p.148).[15]

Just as the Jungian unconscious is timeless and contains childhood experiences as though they were present, the Spielmann's relationship to reality is also characterized in numerous places as too slow, and it is mentioned that he has no watch (p.158). This reinforces the idea that he represents a childhood stage of personality carried over into old age. Significantly, it also characterizes a major difficulty with his music:

> Da er nun zugleich die Dissonanzen so kurz als möglich abtat, überdies die für ihn zu schweren Passagen, von denen er aus Gewissenhaftigkeit nicht eine Note fallen ließ, in einem gegen das Ganze viel zu langsamen Zeitmaß vortrug, so kann man sich wohl leicht eine Idee von der Verwirrung machen, die daraus hervorging. (P.157)[16]

In a significant recent contribution to the criticism of the story, Peter Schäublin has focused attention on the music of the Spielmann, where he discovers, among other things, both the distortion into atemporality and the lack of unity as principles central not only to the music, but to the work. He also relates these two principles to one another:

> Es genügt, sich zu vergegenwärtigen, daß mit der Sekunde als Urdissonanz [an interval the Spielmann avoids playing] die Zweiheit entsteht und daß mit der Zweiheit der Eintritt in die Zeit, in die Geschichte vollzogen wird.[17]

The narrator represents this normal temporal progression, as Schäublin sees it, and the Spielmann, in his music, expresses "Regression" (p.45). All of this supports a specifically Jungian view of the Spielmann as the gifted, unconscious childhood personality juxtaposed to the libido-impoverished adult ego in the narrator. While one is reluctant to project twentieth-century concepts upon Grillparzer, it would be equally dangerous to deny him *a priori* all psychological insights, however vaguely understood, that achieved public status at a later date. Freud and Jung invented neither psychological phenomena nor psychological insight, and in fact supplemented their clinical observations with insights they had gathered from poets such as Grillparzer.

All of these levels—our typology of oppressed child versus emancipated adult, the Christ symbolism, and a Jungian Conscious versus Unconscious—are mutually consistent here and mutually reinforcing. None of these perspectives alone can do justice to the evidence. It is not clear, however, just how Grillparzer conceptualized all this material.

One specifically Grillparzerian dimension nevertheless does emerge from among these issues. We have not yet discussed the causes or origin of the suffering and broken existence of the Spielmann, apart from the paternal indifference and the religious symbolism. The fact of the split self is interpretatively crucial in an immediate formalistic context; so far, however, in the works already discussed it appears to serve also as a gateway to the largely hidden significance of the work as an expression of the poet's personality. This significance—whether Goethe's loss of childhood, Lenz's self-destructive reality, or Klinger's Oedipal theme—so far has served to provide a deeper, individual dimension beneath the common Jungian archetype we have hypothesized. It also provides the individual poets with a unitary theme and foundation for the duality of the split self. We should consider, too, whether Grillparzer also realized this underlying significance in the works under discussion.

Grillparzer in fact developed the concrete psychological character of the Spielmann's "problem" and of the narrator's distance from him—or at least he touched upon it:

"Ich hasse die weibischen Männer" (p.177), Barbara informs Jakob. Kafka, at least, apparently drew the conclusion that the Spielmann's form of love is masochistic. We see this in "Die Verwandlung" which contains the borrowings of the kiss through the glass and the butcher's helper, as Heinz Politzer has noted,[18] and which Kafka also based on Leopold von Sacher-Masoch's *Venus im Pelz*. Thus the Spielmann enjoys the blow delivered by Barbara (p.175). (To be sure, so also did Werther enjoy the box on the ear from Lotte.) Kafka apparently recognized in his "Fleischergeselle" that the butcher hints of an opposite sadism. This barely suggested theme accounts for the total paternal rejection that results when he is seen in Barbara's shop. Masochism also adds substance to the suggestion of yielding, against inhibition, to a forbidden desire (at the description of the festival, p.147). Finally, this problem is commensurate with the chief themes associated with Christ: love, suffering, and rejection (by mankind). Grillparzer, not being Kafka, did not plumb the depths of this form of sexuality.

But both he and Kafka saw that the self-abnegation of masochism is only part of a larger problem of ego. Only suggestions of this are built explicitly into the text, such as Barbara's contemptuous, if unconscious, comparison of the Spielmann to a rotten pea: "Es ist ein Herr aus der Kanzlei, erwiderte sie, indem sie eine wurmstichige Erbse etwas weiter als die anderen von sich warf" (p.169).[19]

While such explicit suggestions of a theme of threat to the ego are quite sparse, the general absurdity of the Spielmann's role in society implicitly inspires a powerful emotional reaction of vicarious ego-assertion in the reader—and all the more so in light of the failure of the narrator to step out from behind his self-protective distance and objectivity to do so. Kafka creates much the same atmosphere, only with greater intensity, in "Die Verwandlung" and in *Das Schloß*, where the absurdity of the social environment and the surveyor's low status encourage the reader inwardly to reject and transcend an intolerable and humiliating world.

III

If the themes of masochism and ego-assertion are so subtle and implicit that they raise serious doubts about the accuracy of this analysis—and indeed they cannot be said to be truly realized in "Der arme Spielmann"—confirmation of both themes can be found in *Die Jüdin von Toledo*. In significant respects this play is the public, dramatic counterpart to the more private genre of the short story. Based loosely on Lope de Vega's *Las paces de los reyes y Judia de Toledo*, *Die Jüdin von Toledo* presents a medieval Spanish King Alfonso who, in the midst of a Moorish threat to his kingdom, succumbs to the attractions of the young Jewess Rahel. He indulges his infatuation temporarily, only to feel his royal dignity ebb and to experience rejection by his court. Finally, Rahel is murdered by members of the court and Alfonso returns to royal propriety. In the end, however, he abdicates in an attempt to resolve the conflict between social duty and deeper human emotions.

The relationship between the two works is close enough to contain a number of specific motifs common to both. King Alfonso describes himself explicitly, for example, as a "child grown into adulthood" ("großgewachsnes Kind"),[20] lending support to the suggestion that Grillparzer may have consciously conceived the function of the Spielmann in such terms. Similarly, our connection of the Spielmann's rejection by society with his Christ function is paralleled in Don Alfonso's view of contemporary Christianity:

> Wir [Christians] kreuzgen täglich zehenmal den Herrn/ durch unsre Sünden, unsre Missetaten,/ Und jene [Jews] habens einmal nur getan. (P.468)[21]

A split self also occurs in the play, if less prominently than in the story. As the central figure the king unites others in his personality:

> Denn wer mich einen König nennt, bezeichnet/ Als Höchsten unter vielen mich, und Menschen/ Sind so ein Teil von meinem eignen Selbst. (P.454)[22]

Other passages show that this is more than mere social metaphor. Specifically, Garceran represents the childhood, with its attendant lack of restraint and uninhibited nature—

something the king never experienced. This aspect is a rather Jungian "energy" ("Kraft") juxtaposed to the "propriety" ("Sitte") of the surrogate father Manrique:

> *Manrique.* Die Kraft war mit der Sitte sonst vereint,/ Doch wurden sie in jüngster Zeit sich feind./ Die Kraft blieb bei der Jugend, wo sie war,/ Die Sitte floh zum altergrauen Haar./ Nehmt meinen Arm. Wie schwankend auch die Schritte:/ Die Kraft entfloh, doch treulich hielt die Sitte. (P.496)[23]

In other words, both principles were harmoniously united with the person of the king, until the latter succumbed to the attractions of Rahel, appropriately aided by Garceran. It is the king, however, who makes decisions, rather than yielding control either to *Kraft* or to *Sitte.* This constellation anticipates the Freudian id (Garceran, if only in the one respect of *Kraft*), superego (Manrique), and ego (Alfonso). When Garceran yields to the authority of Manrique, however, the king is left deserted by his entire court. This pattern is strikingly reminiscent of Klinger's *Grisaldo.* Where the latter work proved a dead end for Klinger, one would like to have handed him Grillparzer's play with the explanation that this may be what he was trying to do. It is not known whether Grillparzer was familiar with Klinger's play; if so, we would have to suspect an influence.[24] Parallel to Klinger's Truffaldino and also resembling Barbara's father in "Der arme Spielmann," the rascally Isak emerges as the king's representative in matters of state—a perversion in public to match the king's perversion in private.

The Klinger-like impoverishment of the king as ego, deserted by the harmony or balance of his representative attributes, appears to find concrete symbolization in the motif of the lame leg, either of man or horse, the animal whose healthy leg mythologically represents libido.[25] When the king is deserted by Garceran, his horse goes lame:

> Der Braune, sagst du, hinkt? Nun es ging scharf./ Doch hab ich seiner fürder nicht vonnöten./ Laß ihn am Zügel führen nach Toledo,/ Dort stellt ihn Ruh als beste Heilung her. (P.496)[26]

Alfonso cries out for a horse as the symbol of what has been taken from him:

> Mein Pferd! Mein Pferd!/ *Knappe.* Man hat die Pferde sämtlich weggebracht,/ Mit sich geführt, vielleicht gejagt ins Freie./ Die Ställe sind geleert, so wie das Schloß. (P.504)[27]

The idea of drawing psychic energy from a biological level is expressed elsewhere in the play:

> Denn wie der Baum mit lichtentfernten Wurzeln/ Die etwa trübe Nahrung saugt tief aus dem Boden,/ So scheint der Stamm, der Weisheit wird gennant/ Und der dem Himmel eignet mit den Ästen,/ Kraft und Bestehn aus trübem Irdischen,/ Dem Fehler nah Werwandten aufzusaugen. (P.456)[28]

A similar motif of the lame leg is seen in the two beggars—one an old man, one a child (suggesting the Spielmann's dual nature as childhood self and old man) and both lame—that accompany the narrator's first sight of the Spielmann (*op.cit.*, p.149). But Grillparzer does not imply—as the mythological or Jungian symbolism requires and as already represented, for example, by Goethe's Mephisto—that the laming of the leg represents loss of libido. Despite the essentially positive reference to "Kraft . . . *aus trübem Irdischen,*" this energy is too threatening to (the bourgeois?) Grillparzer to appear as healthy. Thus the symbolism is inverted. The laming effect is apparently associated not with the inhibition but with the emergence of sexuality in the king's life.

At the beginning Rahel embraces his knee: "*Sie wirft sich vor dem Könige nieder, seinen rechten Fuß umklammernd.*" (p.460)[29]

When finally free, Alfonso shows the effect:

> *Mit dem Fuß auftretend.* Hielt sie den Fuß mir doch so eng umklammert,/ Daß er fast schmerzt.—Im Grunde wunderlich. (P.463)[30]

Elsewhere Grillparzer accounts for this apparent contradiction of the mythological significance by equating the right hand with matters of reason; i.e., of consciousness and ego, as opposed to feeling or heart, or to libido (if we can transpose this sense from the right hand to the right foot):

> *König.* Nicht beide Hände!/ Die Rechte nur, obgleich dem Herzen ferner,/ Gibt man zum Pfand von Bündnis und Vertrag. /Vielleicht um anzudeuten, nicht nur das Gefühl,/ Das seinen Sitz im Herzen aufgeschlagen,/ Auch der Verstand, des Menschen ganzes Wollen/ Muß Dauer geben dem, was man versprach./ Denn wechselnd wie die Zeit ist das Gefühl./ Was man erwogen bleibt in seiner Kraft. (P.498)[31]

The mention of Rahel's clinging specifically to Alfonso's *right* foot suggests that the same sense extends to the leg. Further, this passage underscores that the laming effect has more to do with will and ego than with a Jungian libido, despite the explicit mention of something like the latter concept, as noted above. It is worth observing that the right side of the body is governed by the left hemisphere of the brain, the seat of verbal consciousness and related social behavior, including moral precepts. Grillparzer appears intuitively—or perhaps only accidentally?—to have synthesized the libido symbolism of the leg with the laming of left-hemispheric functions. In the process, however, the specific idea of the emergence of a positive, healthy vitality, explicitly formulated elsewhere in the text, is sacrificed in this symbolism in favor of the inhibition of the conscious, moral personality. Grillparzer's complicated manipulation of this symbol is symptomatic of the conflict that the entire problem appears to have released in him as a dramatist.

The reason for the difficult and threatening quality of this material is the same one that was (barely) suggested in "Der arme Spielmann." Thus the Biblical Jacob (cf. the Spielmann Jakob) is mentioned in the play as having *served* Rahel: "Von Jakob der um Rahel dienend freite—"(p.467).[32] At the beginning the king is "captured" by Rahel (p.461). If these direct suggestions of masochism are muted, the theme of sadomasochism as a whole is not. Rahel's treatment of Alfonso's picture leaves no doubt as to *her* role in this relationship:

> Rück mir den Schemmel her, ich bin die Königin,/ Und diesen König heft ich an den Stuhl./ Die Hexen, sagt man, die zur Liebe zwingen,/ Sie bohren Nadeln, so, in Wachsgebilde,/ Und jeder Stich dringt bis zum Herzen ein/ Und hemmt und fördert wahrgeschaffnes Leben. . . . O, gäbe jeder dieser Stiche Blut,/ Ich wollt es trinken mit den durstgen Lippen/ Und mich erfreun am Unheil, das ich schuf. (P.471)[33]

Later she sounds — ambiguously, to be sure—as though she were giving the king orders in matters relating to the court:

> O weh mir, weh! Bat ich euch denn nicht längst,/ Zu scheiden, Herr, zurückzugehn an Hof/ Und dort zu stören meiner Feinde Trachten./ Allein ihr bliebt. (Pp. 487–88)[34]

But the king is no Spielmann. Like Klinger's king in *Grisaldo*, he is a seat of the ego and cannot simply succumb to the total destruction of his self-image necessary for the masochist to achieve union of self with his mistress. Rahel recognizes this:

> Ich habe nie geliebt. Doch könnt ich lieben,/ Wenn ich in einer Brust den Wahnsinn träfe,/ Der mich erfüllte, wär mein Herz berührt. (P.484)[35]

Don Alfonso indulges only as long as he feels capable of reasserting himself:

> Doch weiß ich auch, daß eines Winkes nur,/ Es eines Worts bedarf, um dieses Trauerspiel *(sic)* Zu lösen in sein eigentliches Nichts. (P.483)[36]

He is only temporarily robbed of the outward layer of his royal self, symbolized by Rahel when she plays with his armor:

> Empört sich der Geliebte und wird stolz,/ Den Helmsturz nieder! *das Visier herablassend* und er steht in Nacht./ Doch wollt er etwa gar sich uns entziehn,/ Schickt' nach dem

Heer-Gerät uns zu verlassen,/ Hinauf mit dem Visier. (Pp. 486–87)[37]

Thus *Die Jüdin von Toledo* is concerned not so much with masochism as with the formidable, barricaded ego that is driven to this extreme form of love as the only means to reach the "Thou." This problem was treated implicitly in "Der arme Spielmann." Here it is the central concern of the play, and it helps Grillparzer to counteract a distasteful and threatening "Wahnsinn."[38] From the beginning the king projects a sovereign willfulness of royal ego:

> *Manrique da alle schweigen.* Herr, du weißt,/ Verboten ist der Eintritt diesem Volk/ In Königs Garten, wenn der Hof zur Stelle. *König.* Nun, wenns verboten, so erlaub ichs denn. (P.461)[39]

When Rahel goes to work on his picture, she removes it from its frame, symbolically releasing Alfonso as a human being from his socially defined ego. As soon as he yields to temptation, he finds himself intolerably threatened by the need to hide from the court:

> Was fällt dir ein!/Soll ich verbergen mich vor meinen Dienern?/ Und doch fürcht ich den Schmerz der Königin. (P.473)[40]
> Muß ich, noch gestern Vorbild aller Zucht,/ Mich heute scheun vor jedes Dieners Blicken? (P.475)[41]

Alphonso's love must be adulterated by the protection afforded by an underlying "contempt" (p.485), even "hatred" (p.483). In the fourth act his self-assertion culminates in an attitude of moral omnipotence: "Ich spreche mich von meinen Sünden los" (p.499).[42] Equally dubious is his subordination of nature to society: "Natürlich ist zuletzt nur was erlaubt" (p.869).[43] This courtly stance is contradicted by his more impressive summation to Esther:

> Ich sage dir, wir sind nur Schatten/ Ich, du, und jene andern aus der Menge./ Denn bist du gut; du hast es so gelernt,/ . . . Sie aber war die Wahrheit, ob verzerrt,/ All,

was sie tat, ging aus ihrem Selbst,/ Urplötzlich, unverhofft und ohne Beispiel. (P.509)[44]

Thus the play vacillates. Alfonso's recognition of the validity of libido (Kraft aus dem Irdischen) and his indulgence of Rahel give way to a reassertion of ego. This, in turn, is followed by the desire to punish Rahel's murderers and by affirmation of her more intense reality. A dubious one-sided assertion of "Sitte" then follows, finally countered by Esther's superior, humbling admonishment:

Ich aber sage dir, du stolzer König:/ Geh hin, geh hin in prunkendem Vergessen./ Du hältst dich frei von meiner Schwester Macht,/ Weil abgestumpft der Stachel ihres Eindrucks. (P.517)[45]

Unable, apparently, to reconcile the conflicting values of social ego and sexual nature, Grillparzer seeks refuge in Alfonso's withdrawal from both, giving up Rahel and abdicating in favor of his son. This hardly is a solution to the problem, for it leads only to a realization of man's weakness and to a general *nostra culpa:*

Esther. Dann nehm rück den Fluch den ich gesprochen,/ Dann seid ihr schuldig auch, und ich und sie./ Wir stehn gleich jenen in der Sünder Reihe,/ Verzeihn wir denn, damit uns Gott verzeihe. (P.518)[46]

It is significant that these final lines are spoken by Esther and not by the king. One does not have the impression that he is embarrassed and speechless. He has, after all, saved his honor and dignity by yielding the throne. Rather, we sense that these alternating positions have finally nullified his personality as a voice for the poet; that Grillparzer must ultimately leave him aside and find a relatively unscathed person to express his final statement.

The larger sphere of these two (thematically, at least) mutually orbiting works thus affords a coherence only marginally and suggestively available in either one alone. The theme of the split self, so clearly realized in "Der arme Spielmann," appears largely to lack the sort of explanation supplied by the hobby-horse scene of *Die Räuber* or Goethe's autobiographical concerns in *Götz*. But the underlying themes of ego and masochism, only subtly suggested, lead outward and grow into certainties that are firmly anchored and developed in *Die Jüdin von Toledo*. There, conversely, the theme of the split self as such is easily overlooked. In Grillparzer's work, the split self emerges as a concrete, if disguised, outward manifestation of an inner, emotional problem of self and sexuality that he apparently found most difficult and dangerous to share with a Metternichian society.

Notes

1. Richard Brinkmann, *Wirklichkeit und Illusion. Studien über Gehalt und Grenzen des Begriffs Realismus für die erzählende Dichtung des 19. Jahrhunderts* (Tübingen: Max Niemeyer, 1957), pp.87–145. Heinz Politzer, *Franz Grillparzers "Der arme Spielmann"* (Dichtung und Erkenntnis, 2: Stuttgart: Metzler, 1967).

2. John M. Ellis, *Narration in the German Novelle* (Angelica Germanica Series, 2. Cambridge: Cambridge University Press, 1974).

3. Günther Jungbluth, "Franz Grillparzer's Erzählung 'Der arme Spielmann.' Ein Beitrag zu ihrem Verstehen," *Orbis Litterarum* 24(9) (1969): 35–51.

4. Eleonore Frey-Staiger, *Grillparzer: Gestalt und Gestaltung des Traums* (Zürcher Beiträge zur deutschen Literatur und Geistesgeschichte, 26: Zürich: Atlantis Verlag, 1966).

5. Franz Grillparzer, *Sämtliche Werke*, vol. 3; ed. Peter Frank and Karl Pörnbacher (Munich: Carl Hanser, 1964), p.156. All quotations from Grillparzer's works are taken from this edition.

6. "Parts of the whole . . . in which in the final analysis the God-principle resides— . . . "

7. "In Vienna a folk festival—if ever a festival has deserved this name—is held on the Sunday after the full moon in the month of July of each year, together with the following day. The people attend and give it themselves; and if the higher classes appear, they do so only in their capacity as members of the people. There is no possibility of separation. . . . "

8. " . . . as one who loves people, I say, particularly when they forget as a group their individual concerns for a time and feel themselves as parts of a whole in which in the final analysis the God-principle resides— . . . . "

9. " . . . as such a person I find each folk festival a veritable soul-festival, a pilgrimage, a religious devotion."

10. " . . . and thus he belabored an old, cracked violin, whereby he marked the rhythm not only by tapping his foot, but simultaneously with a corresponding movement of his entire bent body. But all the efforts to bring unity into his work were fruitless."

11. Wolfgang Paulsen, *Die Ahnfrau. Zu Grillparzers früher Dramatik* (Tübingen: Max Niemeyer, 1962). Cf. also Joachim Müller, "Grillparzer und Goethe. Grillparzers Goetheverständnis und Goethe-Bild," *Chronik des Wiener Goethe-Vereins* 74 (1970); 30–57. For Grillparzer's reaction to *Götz*, p.32.

12. Zdenko Škreb has discussed the importance of the fairy tale for Grillparzer, as

he was influenced by such institutions as the Viennese *Volksbühne* and such poets as Calderon and Lope de Vega ("Das Märchenspiel bei Grillparzer," *Jahrbuch der Grillparzer-Gesellschaft*, dritte Folge 7 [1967]: 37 – 55). Škreb also emphasizes Grillparzer's sensitivity to unconscious psychological material contained in fairy-tale sources and motifs—but unfortunately without discussing "Der arme Spielmann."

13. "I fell on my knees and prayed aloud and couldn't understand how, in my childhood, I once had thought so little of—yes, actually hated—the dear God, and kissed the violin and pressed it to my heart and played on and on."

14. Hedwig von Roques-von Beit, *Symbolik des Märchens. Versuch einer Deutung*, 2 vols. (Bern: Francke Verlag, 1960).

15. " . . . and indeed, one cannot understand famous men if one has not deeply comprehended the obscure."

16. "He did away with the dissonances as quickly as possible. In addition he played the passages too difficult for him much too slowly in comparison to the rest—and conscientiously insisted on playing every note. Thus one can get an idea of the resulting confusion."

17. "It is enough to remember that duality arises with the second as the basic dissonance [an interval the Spielmann avoids playing—P. W.] and that with duality the entrance is made into time, into history" (Peter Schäublin, "Das Musizieren des armen Spielmanns. Zu Grillparzers musikalischer Zeichensprache," *Sprachkunst 3* [1972]: 31 – 55).

18. Heinz Politzer, *Franz Kafka: der Künstler* (Frankfurt a/M : S. Fischer, 1965): 122 – 23.

19. " 'It's a gentleman from the chancery,' she replied, flicking away a worm-eaten pea a bit farther than the others."

20. *Sämtliche Werke (op.cit.)*, vol.2 (1970), p.466.

21. "We [Christians] crucify the Lord/ Ten times each day through sins, our misdeeds,/ And they [Jews] did it but once."

22. "For he who calls me King, selects/ Me from the crowd as highest, and they/ Are thus a part of my own self."

23. "*Manrique*. Vitality was One with moral custom,/ Yet now they have become antagonists./ Vitality remained with youth, as then/ While moral custom fled to graying head./ Take my arm. However weak the stride,/ Vitality has gone, but custom's true."

24. Fritz Martini has recently compared Klinger's *Simsone Grisaldo* with Grillparzer's *Ein treuer Diener seines Herrn* ("Die treuen Diener ihrer Herrn. Zu F.M. Klinger and F. Grillparzer," *Jahrbuch der Grillparzer Gesellschaft* 12 [1976]: 147 – 77). Although unable to establish concrete evidence of Klinger's influence on Grillparzer, Martini finds a significant similarity in the treatment of the theme of court intrigue. It is worth nothing here that Grillparzer also included a clear, if undeveloped, motif of the unity of Gertrude and Otto in *Ein treuer Diener:* "Ein Knabe wünscht ich mir zu sein—wie Otto./ Er wuchs heran, in ihm war ich ein Jüngling,/ . . . Er ist mein Ich, er ist der Mann Gertrude,/ Ich bitt euch, trennt mich nicht von meinem Selbst" (*Grillparzer Werke*, ed. Paul Stapf, 2 vols. (Berlin and Darmstadt: Der Tempel-Verlag, 1959), 1: 471 – 72).

25. Cf. the discussion of this concept in connection with Broch's use of the motif below, pp. 163–164.

26. "The brown one limps, you say? 'Twas run quite hard./ But now I have no further need for it./ To Toledo let the horse be led./ There give it rest as best of all the cures."

27. "My horse! My horse! *Page*. They took them all away,/ Took them along, perhaps drove off to wander./ The stalls have been deserted, the castle too."

28. "For as the tree with darkly buried roots/ Draws sustenance deep from the ground beneath,/ So seems the trunk, with wisdom oft compared,/ And with its branches suitable for heaven,/ To suck vitality and lastingness/ Not far from fault and error."

29. *"She throws herself down in front of the King, embracing his right foot."*

30. *"Stepping about on his foot.* She held my foot so tightly/ It almost hurts:—In truth it is quite strange."

31. *"King.* Not both hands!/ The right alone, though farther from the heart,/ One gives as pledge of unity agreed./ Perhaps to say, not feeling by itself,/ Which in the heart its seat has well established,/ But reason too, a person's total will/ Must give a lastingness to pledge of faith./ For feeling vacillates like time itself./ What one has weighed stays in validity."

32. "Of Jacob who courted Rahel serving."

33. "Give me that stool, I am the Queen,/ I pin this King to it./ The witches, they say, who force a man to love,/ They plunge the needles, so, in waxen figures,/ And every jab sinks deep into the heart/ And holds and summons true-created life. . . . O if each piercing thrust released his blood,/ I'd drink it eagerly with thirsty lips,/ Delight myself in harm that I inflicted."

34. "O woe is me! Did I not long since ask/ My Lord, that you return at once to court?/ To wreck the scheming of my enemies./ And yet you stayed."

35. "I have not ever loved. Yet I could love,/ Were I to find in lover's heart the madness/ Fulfilling me, then would my heart be touched."

36. "Yet I know well, a gesture merely, a word/ Suffices well, this dream-play to dissolve/ Into its proper nothingness."

37. "Should the lover revolt and proudly stand,/ The visor down! *(lowering the visor)* and then he stands in night./ Yet if he wished to go from us away,/ Sent off to find the army and to leave,/ The visor up again."

38. Cf. Wolfgang Paulsen's discussion of the underlying emotional significance of the play for Grillparzer, and its reflection of his affair with Marie von Smolenitz ("Nachwort" to *Die Jüdin von Toledo* [Universalbibliothek no. 4394; Stuttgart: Reclam, 1968], especially pp.74–78).

39. *"Manrique, since all are silent.* Lord, you know/ Forbidden is the entrance to this people/ Into the royal park, when court is here./ *King.* Well, if forbidden, I permit it then."

40. "What are you thinking of?/ Should I secret myself from my own servants?/ And yet I fear the Queen's embarrassment."

41. "But yesterday a model of good breeding,/ Must I retreat from every servant's glances?"

42. "I free myself from sins by me committed."

43. "Natural is only what's permitted."

44. "I say to you, we're only shadows/ I and you and all the others there./ For if you're good; you've merely learned it so,/ . . . But she was truth, perhaps herself distorted,/ All that she did, went out from inner being./ At once, unique and unexpectedly."

45. "But I now say to you, you pompous King:/ Go forth, go forth in proud forgetfulness./ You hold away the power of my sister/ Because the sting of her effect is dulled."

46. *"Esther.* Then I take back the curse that I have spoken,/ Then you are guilty too, and I—and she./ We stand like them in ranks of sinners jointly./ Let us forgive, that God forgive us too."

Frank Wedekind: *Der Marquis von Keith* and Walter Hasenclever: *Der Sohn*

I

H. MACCLEAN has demonstrated that Frank Wedekind's *Der Marquis von Keith* (1900) centers around the dual selves of Keith and his childhood friend Ernst Scholz, and that the model for the former was Goethe's Mephisto.[1] In the published version of the play the chief evidence pointing to *Faust* is the symbol of the lame leg, characteristic both of Keith and, temporarily, Scholz. But the earlier versions, as MacClean shows, contain numerous explicit and implicit reflections of Goethe's play. MacClean extends the analysis by bridging from Wedekind to Nietzsche. Otherwise this tracing of the relationship to *Faust* serves well as a foundation and point of departure for our present concern. To be sure, it is necessary to complement MacClean's essay with an earlier observation of Wedekind's friend and biographer Artur Kutscher before proceeding. Kutscher saw and formulated the problem of the split self in the work:

> Wedekind nennt sein Stück "das Wechselspiel zwischen einem Don Quixote des Lebensgenußes und einem Don Quixote der Moral." Dieser letztere, Ernst Scholz, ist nicht nur ersterem zum Gegenbilde geschaffen, sondern beide sind aus des Dichters Dualismus geboren und haben ein-

ander bestimmt. Eine Einheit ist hier zerlegt worden in ihre Extreme, die beiden Seelen einer Brust.[2]

Among the works examined so far, Wedekind's play represents the most intricate and most intensive treatment of the split-self theme. Much of the dramatist's enigmatic language crystalises suddenly here into the clear-cut logic of a battle of part-selves for survival.

Wedekind's unique relationship to the problem was influenced by the unusual fact that his own emancipation from his father—with whom he had come to physical violence (Kutscher, p.46)—at first failed miserably. He was forced, rather insincerely, to beg forgiveness in order to obtain financial help. This disastrous situation was corrected only by his father's sudden death, which freed him both psychologically and financially, but which also must have left its permanent mark on him. This is artistically reflected in the fact that a Keith-like emancipated figure recurs throughout Wedekind's work.

Keith is the central figure of the play, the seat of the ego. He is the perfect archetype of the emancipated personality— full of contemptuous wit and cynical of love and emotions. Like Mephisto, he recognizes only the sensual side of love. Characteristically, he has traveled abroad in America and describes how he has been "whipped from land to land."[3] He admits that he had been born a cripple and a beggar, but not a slave (p.18). He limps as a symbol of his isolation from natural energies. Therefore he warns young Hermann Casimir not to follow in his footsteps:

> Durch das wirkliche Erleben verlieren Sie nur die Fähig-keiten, die Sie in Ihrem Fleisch und Blut mit auf die Welt gebracht haben. Das gilt ganz speziell von Ihnen, dem Sohn und einstigen Erben unseres größten deutschen Finanzgenies. (P.7)[4]

As a second physical symbol of Keith's condition, his "crude red hands of a clown" (p.5) suggest a flaw in his polished social armor, the sham of his confidence game.

Keith is in fact an even purer model of the emancipated

type than Mephisto. Wedekind recognized in this personality not only the devil, but the Prodigal Son. The latter motif is mentioned explicitly, if only indirectly through its application to Police Inspector Raspe (a secondary version of the split self here):

> *Scholz.* Er erzählte mir, er sei ursprünglich Theologe gewesen, habe aber durch zu vieles Studieren seinen Glauben verloren und ihn dann auf dem Wege wiederzufinden gesucht, auf dem der verlorene Sohn seinen Glauben wiedererfand. (P.30)[5]

That this motif is also aimed at Keith is evident from the way he wastes money and lavishes it on the three artists, when he desperately needs to cover his obligations to the investors in the "Fairy Palace" *(Feenpalast)*. Wedekind's own designation of Keith as a "Don Quixote of life's pleasure" essentially reflects the social dimension of this personality and the rebellion against the prudish bourgeois sexual mores of his time. But it does not exhaust his psychological significance as the emancipated type, supported by the models of Mephisto and the Prodigal Son.

The character of Keith's counterpart, Ernst Scholz, once again raises the question of an earlier versus an alternate self. As a "Don Quixote of morality," Scholz negates the social rebellion of Keith. In part he represents the paternal values Keith has left behind. In contrast to his friend he is wealthy— heir to a paternal fortune. He is notably capable of love, but (like the Spielmann) repels Anna, the woman he desires and must win if he is to be successful. Although he describes himself as having been at one time like a prisoner—presumably in his subservience to paternal values—he now feels himself free in his emulation of Keith:

> Aber sehen Sie, ich bin ja so glücklich wie ein Mensch, der von frühester Kindheit auf im Kerker gelegen hat und der nun zum erstenmal in seinem Leben freie Luft atmet. (P.58)[6]

Scholz is thus a good example of the oppressed self. His ability to love is emphasized symbolically by his wealth, a

counter symbol to Keith's extravagant poverty. He suspects
that his fortune—representing the father—is the cause of his
suffering, a suggestion which the envious Keith, aghast, calls
"blasphemy" (p.25). Thus Scholz's money suggests both his
capability (i.e., ability to love) and the price he must pay for it
(paternal oppression), whereas Keith's inability to hold on to
money and his desperate need for it express his corresponding
inability to love. MacClean asserts that Keith and Scholz are
not actually alter egos, but only complementary figures
(p.165). This is true only in the most superficial sense that
they are not doubles. Both are twenty-seven years old and
shared a common childhood. Specifically, both were influenced by Keith's father, and in a manner predictable from
their emancipation or lack of the same:

> *v. Keith.* Mein Vater war so selbstlos und gewissenhaft, wie
> es der Hauslehrer und Erzieher eines Grafen Trautenau
> [Scholz] nun einmal sein muß. Du warst sein Musterknabe,
> und ich war sein Prügeljunge. (P.24)[7]

The fact that Scholz is now attempting to follow Keith would
logically have to disturb the father:

> *v. Keith.* Mein Vater würde sich vor Schreck im Grabe
> umkehren bei dem Gedanken, daß du—mich um meinen
> Rat bittest. (P.23)[8]

Scholz's reply hints at the identity of their fathers:

> Dein Vater hat redlich sein Teil zu meiner einseitigen
> geistigen Entwicklung beigetragen. (P.24)[9]

As in *Die Räuber*, a key incident appears to symbolize the
event of the splitting of the personality. As one can recon-
struct from the superficially irrelevant dates and times scattered throughout the play, both Keith and Scholz suffered a
catastrophe at about the same time; i.e., three years earlier.
Keith was captured in Cuba and shot—significantly as a revo-
lutionary—along with twelve other conspirators. Meanwhile
Scholz was employed by a railroad, where he set up a
regulation that could not be followed:

Ich hatte ein Bahnreglement geändert. Es lag eine beständige Gefahr darin, daß dieses Bahnreglement unmöglich genau respektiert werden konnte. Meine Befürchtungen waren natürlich übertrieben, aber mit jedem Tage sah ich das Unglück näherkommen. Mir fehlt eben das seelische Gleichgewicht, das dem Menschen aus einem menschenwürdigen Familienheim erwächst.—Am ersten Tage nach Einführung meines neuen Reglements erfolgte ein Zusammenstoß von zwei Schnellzügen, der neun Männern, drei Frauen und zwei Kindern das Leben kostete. (P.22)[10]

If the two children are equated with Keith and Scholz as parts of one self, then both disasters take twelve lives in addition to the self. Keith, incidentally, is sometimes taken for a "railroad baron" (p.6). In psychic terms, the strict moral standard that Scholz (as superego?) imposed upon the personality could not be met, and the Keith-side was seemingly destroyed. But Keith claims to have arisen as from the dead:

Ich falle natürlich auf den ersten Schuß und bleibe tot, bis man mich beerdigen will. Seit jenem Tage fühle ich mich erst wirklich als den Herrn meines Lebens.[11]

He concludes by denying precisely the principle of duty represented by Scholz and imposed in his "Bahnreglement":

(Aufspringend): Verpflichtungen gehen wir bei unserer Geburt nicht ein, und mehr als dieses Leben wegwerfen kann man nicht. Wer nach seinem Tode noch weiterlebt, der steht über den Gesetzen. (P.21)[12]

Scholz and Keith are both struggling to unite emancipation and the ability to love, each from a different, opposing position. In this respect Scholz is more an alternate than an earlier self. He can be seen therefore as a "half person" (p.22), insofar as he has manifested (until now, as he sees it) only part of the personality. However, as a potential unifier of the personality he also contains "two souls" (p.45). In order to unify the self Scholz at first appears to be willing to yield his own separate identity to Keith. He admits to failure, asks to be made into a "man of pleasure" (p.24), gives himself up to

Keith's "direction" (pp. 19–20), and offers to make his money available to his friend. But Scholz is holding something back. He wants to share in Keith's emancipation and still remain "a useful member of society" (p.75). This suggests that he intends to unify the personality from his perspective, not Keith's. Thus he attempts to play the guitar in order to acquire an artistic mentality, and learns to ride a bicycle expressly as a source of greater freedom.

At the celebration of the formation of the group of businessmen ("Karyatiden") which is to help Keith build the *Feenpalast,* Scholz is wounded in the knee by the largest firecracker, loaded—as Keith warns more than once—"with all of hell" (p.52). This event symbolizes Scholz's metamorphosis into a Keith-like personality. Afterward he demands the hand of Anna, crucial to the success of his attempt to synthesize love and emancipation. But Scholz's remodeling of character is too facile, too willful and symbolic. It is not a simple matter to integrate two opposing personalities. Anna indeed is not convinced and rejects him now as before, whereupon Scholz, on the verge of a breakdown, gives up his limp and with it his attempt to emulate Keith. The latter, meanwhile, has his own plan to unify the self. For him the task is to return home somehow and regain love. Both needs are united in the project for the *Feenpalast,* which symbolizes a home and requires money: i.e., love, for its achievement. Keith states explicitly that the significance of this project is symbolic: "Der Feenpalast dient mir nur als Sammelplatz meiner Kräfte" (p.11).[13] He also expresses the desire to regain a home, one suggestive of a castle:

> Ich habe ein wechselvolles Leben hinter mir, aber jetzt denke ich doch ernstlich daran, mir ein Haus zu bauen; ein Haus mit möglichst hohen Gemächern, mit Park und Freitreppe . . . Mit der Vergangenheit habe ich abgeschlossen und sehne mich nicht zurück. (P.12)[14]

Here, too, as with Scholz's efforts, a contradictory element cannot be eliminated. He cannot cut himself off from his past and also return home. Thus the *Feenpalast* is very close to a *Luftschloß* and in fact is brought into closest linguistic proximity with this idea: ". . . dann sprenge ich den Feenpalast samt Aufsichtsrat und Aktionärversammlung—in die Luft!" (p.87)[15]

The chief obstacle to Keith's success is not Scholz, who also wishes the reunification of the self. True, Scholz's interest and intention may exclude this being done according to Keith's plan, but this aspect of the conflict of two part-selves is not developed. For Keith it is Konsul Casimir who holds the key to success. Casimir is an obvious father figure, significantly a "financial genius" whose participation, logically enough, is crucial to the success of the project. Keith is attempting to win over the father figure purely on his own terms, utilizing his emancipated chicanery to the fullest. In a manner characteristic of his attempt to force reality to conform to his will, he falsely claims Casimir's support. When he is discovered, the project collapses. Casimir also robs Keith of Anna when she accepts his offer of marriage—a particularly disturbing blow for Keith in view of the father so close to the surface in Casimir. Anna is the attractive, emancipated woman Keith finds interesting, even though he cannot actually love her. As symbolized by her name, "Werdenfels" ("become rock"), she is as incapable of love as he is. The counterpart to Anna is Molly, Keith's common-law wife. Her name suggests an opposite softness. She bores and irritates Keith, serving mainly to bring to full expression the emotional sterility of his personality.

All of the remaining male figures (except the "Karyatiden") represent various stages of development of the self, secondary to the immediate split between Keith and Scholz. The youngest is Sascha, aged thirteen, Keith's errand boy. While only minimally developed, he is significant for the attention given to his dress in the stage directions; specifically to his "knee breeches" (p.13), and later his "satin knee breeches" (p.52). This may be intended to highlight the healthy leg, as opposed to Keith's limp, and presumably a healthy libido characteristic of the child stage. Throughout the last act Keith calls in vain for Sascha, who has been taken away by Anna. The repeated calls for someone obviously not there, at a time when Keith is suffering a series of psychic blows, take on a symbolic ring, suggesting Sascha's function for Keith as a vicarious source of psychic health or energy (to use Keith's own term: "Nonsense, I have no energy at all," he asserts, p.10). Of course, Sascha's presence, like the tricks both Keith and Scholz employ to grasp for a unity of self, is only window dressing, and Anna's burglarizing him away little more than an arabesque in Keith's fall. Temporally more closely related to Keith and Scholz is Hermann Casimir, fifteen years old and on the verge of emancipating himself. He serves to bring out the father in the consul. Desiring to follow Keith, he is advised by the latter to consider what he is leaving behind him: namely the abilities he brought into life (p.7), and to return home. It is significant that Keith warns him not to follow the same course; in doing so, he betrays his true view of his own state. Equally significant is the fact that Hermann's mother died three years earlier; i.e., at the time of Scholz's railroad disaster and Keith's execution. This is a third version or aspect of what is psychically the same event, suggesting that the loss of the mother precipitates the catastrophe of emancipation.

A fourth version is represented by the Police Inspector Raspe, in his early twenties. For him the crucial event was his imprisonment for two years. Originally a theology student, he was incarcerated as though for having abdicated values associated with conscience—the same area of concern as for Scholz (p.30). As a result of imprisonment Raspe has reversed his emancipation. He now represents psychically a stage younger than his years, as is confirmed by his description:

Raspe, anfangs der Zwanziger, in heller Sommertoilette und Strohhut, hat die kindlich-harmlosen Züge eines Guido-Renischen Engels. (P.37)[16]

Raspe's purpose is to exact revenge upon Keith for not having testified at his trial as a "psychiatric expert" (p.67); i.e., as a source of independent rationality and self-justification to counteract the values and influence of the father. Anywhere else one might expect a part-self that had successfully reversed emancipation to be a positive phenomenon, but not in a play by Wedekind. Raspe is just another threat to Keith as the center of ego in the play. Aside from Keith and Hermann, the names of all characters representing some stage or aspect of the self begin with a sibilant. The only exception is Raspe—and his name is an anagram for "Spare!" ("Save"), an exhortation relevant to Keith as Prodigal Son. Raspe thus plays a role close to the personality of Scholz, except that Scholz has decided to follow Keith, whereas Raspe has turned back to the paternal values of society. Raspe's only function in the plot is to blow the whistle on Keith's chicanery, precipitating his downfall.

Beyond Keith in emancipation are the three projections into a dismal future: the artists Zamrjaki, Sommersberg, and Saranieff. Essentially one figure in grotesque, comic triplicate, each of the three possesses attributes that suggest in purely negative terms an intensification of Keith's emancipation. Saranieff enters first, dressed appropriately in black, implying an affinity with death as the ultimate goal of the emancipated. Where Keith has the red hands of a clown, Saranieff wears "fire-engine red gloves" together with "trousers somewhat too short, crude shoes" (p.31). Again attention is focused on the leg, perhaps hinting at something a little like a clubbed foot. Sommersberg enters next. In his late thirties, he conforms to the logic of the ages of the various part-selves. His tattered clothing suggests his impoverishment, both financially and psychically. He wears "torn kid gloves" (p.46). While not significant for his dress, the composer Zamrjaki steps into the limelight only to have his new symphony hooted from the stage. Nothing compensates this extreme emancipation for all that it lacks; not even, apparently, an artistic creativity anyone (including Keith) respects. It is characteristic of Wedekind's style that such bleak prospects are carried to a logical, grotesque extreme. No one supports anyone else, even in a common cause. Thus Saranieff, with underlying, unintended comic reflection on himself, sneers at the entrance of Sommersberg:

Die Gräber tun sich auf! Sommersberg! Und Sie schämen sich nicht, von den Toten aufzuerstehen, um Sekretär dieses Feenpalastes zu werden?! (p.55)[17]

Saranieff also attempts to use Simba, the serving girl, against Keith and Scholz (p.54).

In the last act Keith is systematically deserted or betrayed by everyone. Anna has accepted Casimir's marriage proposal and taken Simba and Sascha along; the three artists have only drained his resources; Raspe has betrayed him to the "Karyatiden" and Casimir; and Scholz, most intimately part of himself, has turned against him. Keith cannot even enjoy a consequential martyrdom, but must also bear the burden of guilt for Molly's suicide. That he nevertheless survives, emancipation intact, if impoverished, promises only future repetitions of the *Feenpalast* disaster. Such prospects must be felt as bitter indeed for a Keith who advised Hermann against following him and who can look forward only to joining the three *Totenvogel* artists.

II

Wedekind did not undertake a further development of the split-self theme. In fact his *Franziska* (1911) suggests a positive unwillingness to deal further with it. An extended analogy to *Faust*, Parts One and Two, this work places the typical Wedekind "wheeler-dealer" Veit Kunz in the role of Mephisto. Kunz functions both as dramatist and actor in his own play-within-a-play (a public acknowledgment of his identification with Wedekind). The Faust figure is Franziska, whom Kunz emancipates from a childhood environment of torment resulting from parental discord. Kunz, for his part, derives "self-confidence"[18] from Franziska's allegiance to him. Since *Keith* contains both significant Faust parallels (particularly in the earlier versions) and a split-self theme, we can safely conclude that Wedekind perceived this relationship between Faust and Mephisto.

But no clear suggestion of a split self can be found in *Franziska*. The closest hint of such a relationship occurs in Franziska's role as Helena in Kunz's play:

> Weißt du, daß *mein* Geschick dem *deinen* glich,/Daß wir, obwohl getrennt durch Ewigkeiten,/Denselben Weg genommen, du und ich? (P.197)[19]

Kunz, recipient of this vague address, appears in "penitent's rags, a cord around the loins" (p.190), but is otherwise unidentified. This is hardly evidence for the split-self theme. Furthermore, at the end Franziska rejects both Kunz and another lover (who has popped up late in the play) as equal rivals. Instead, she turns to an even newer admirer who is devoted to her and her child. In this disjointed and unprepared conclusion Wedekind is, if anything, breaking the split-self bond between Faust and Mephisto. Perhaps he is attempting in this play to escape the tiresome repetition of sterile, emancipated *Totenvögel* by reinvesting his libido in a female protagonist and shunting aside his emancipated artist self in her favor.

Thus Wedekind concentrates his development of the split self in one play, the denouement of which leaves its author trapped in a deadly circle of stubborn emancipation that pits an elastic *Aufspringen* ("springing up") (cf. MacClean's discussion of the circus motif, *op. cit.*) against an inexorable drain of psychic energy. *Franziska* may have been Wedekind's attempt to escape from this circle, not by recanting emancipation, but by stepping out of the conflict altogether. It was not for him but for a disciple to pick up the theme where he had left it at the end of *Keith*.

III

Walter Hasenclever's *Der Sohn* (1914) recapitulates and develops Wedekind's treatment of the split-self in *Der Marquis von Keith*. Here a twenty-year-old "son," abused and imprisoned by his father, escapes with the help of a "friend," delivers a speech at a rally of the "Club for the Preservation of Joy," is brought back to his father in shackles, then, in a final confrontation, causes the latter's death.

Up to a point the work openly imitates *Keith*. A split-self pair directly suggestive of Keith and Scholz dominates the third act. "Cherubim," whose character appears to be approximately the opposite of his name, is about to deliver a speech at the "Club" in an atmosphere reminiscent of Keith's frantic efforts for his *Feenpalast:* "Wenn etwas schief geht, stürzt alles."[20]

Cherubim's project can succeed only with the financial support of his friend von Tuchmeyer, son of a rich industrialist, who has squandered his inheritance upon Cherubim. He decides (like Scholz) "that one can live in spite of one's money" (p.62). Cherubim underscores their common bond and isolates the two of them from their friends: "Es handelt sich doch hier um dich und um mich—deshalb unter vier Augen" (p.63).[21]

In character and—so far as Hasenclever is able—in language these two figures emulate Keith and Scholz. By this means Hasenclever distinctly attaches his play to Wedekind as something of a patron saint of Expressionist drama.

Other motifs from *Keith* include the frequent "jumping up" of various characters and the "friend's" characteristic as "clown" (p.72). The *Faust* parallels may be modeled on Wedekind's procedure in *Keith* and *Franziska*, including a variation on the Easter scene. Here, in iambic pentameter, the son contemplates suicide, then decides to live. A moment later the friend enters, commenting that the son owes his life to a "plagiarism of *Faust*" (p.14). Later the friend uses an interpretation of the sense of Faust's pact with Mephisto; namely that pleasure kills (p.72), to replace the "Club for the Preservation of Joy" with his own movement to abolish the family as a means to free sons from their fathers.[22]

It is in the context of the latter theme that Hasenclever organizes his own split-self pair in the son and the friend. The former, who has been oppressed by his father to the edge of credibility (having been whipped and beaten), at the age of twenty is still not permitted to leave the house in the evening. Echoes—in all probability accidental—of Grillparzer's Spielmann can be heard in the precipitation of the crisis that occurs when the son purposely fails to pass his examinations, along with the domestic incarceration, the impersonal distance of the father, and the son's love of music (p.37). Like the Spielmann, the son represents a childhood personality carried past the normal stages of emancipation; but, unlike the Spielmann, the son finally reacts explosively to this situation.

The first to recognize the split-self in this work, as Wolfgang Paulsen has pointed out, was the psychoanalyst Hans Sachs, in 1919 (*op.cit.*, p.538). Sachs in fact recognized specifically the emancipatory function of the friend. But he also introduced the idea that the friend is a father figure—a strange conclusion that may be the result of an early psychoanalytic tendency to reduce psychological relationships to a few basic patterns, generally parental. This idea has taken root in Paulsen's otherwise authoritative essay. However, evidence for it in the text is insufficient. The fact that the friend betrays to the father the son's whereabouts is not an indication of his father role, as Paulsen concludes. Rather, it is a means to maneuver the son into killing the father. Paulsen sees the son, for whom the friend (as secondary father figure and simultaneously as a projection of the title figure) sacrifices himself, as proceeding into the future as a replica of his "Prussianized" father.

Another difficulty arises when Paulsen, taking a cue from Hasenclever's comment that all figures in the play are seen from the son's perspective, concludes that they are all, like the friend, projections of him (p.534). We should take another look at Hasenclever's preface to the program of the first performance in 1916:

> Dieses Stück wurde im Herbst 1913 geschrieben und hat den Zweck, die Welt zu ändern. Es ist die Darstellung des Kampfes durch die Geburt des Lebens, . . . Der Umweg des Geschöpfes, sein Urbild zu erreichen; . . . es ist die Welt des Zwanzigjährigen, aus der Seele des Einzigen gesehen. Der Versuch, das Gegenspiel der Figuren in demselben Darsteller zu verkörpern, würde die Einheit des Ganzen erläutern: ein Zuschauer, der, dem Parkett und der Bühne entsagend, außerhalb stände, würde erkennen, daß alles, was hier geschieht, nur verschieden ist als Ausdruck des einen gleichen Gedankens.[23]

Neither the "counterplay" of figures in unity nor the unity of *thought* of the entire play quite justifies the extreme conclusion that all figures in the play are one self and might be played by a single actor. The split selves here consist of Cherubim and von Tuchmeyer (as an acknowledgment of Wedekind) and the son and the friend (as Hasenclever's contribution to the theme). The "Urbild" ("model") the son reaches by a detour need not be equated with the father, since nothing in the text suggests such a meeting of minds, but would seem to refer to the emancipated self-realization of the son at the end of the play.

The text poses few difficulties in clarifying the nature of the split-self here. At a time of crisis in the son's life the friend appears, almost as a spirit, and offers his assistance. The friend is slightly older, has traveled abroad, and belongs to the inner circle of the club. He encourages the son to make known to his governess the son's desire for love. The son does so, discovering that she also returns his love with selfless devotion. The friend returns when the son is locked in his room in order to help him escape. As an oppressed earlier self capable of love the son is about to become emancipated and characteristically finds that he must renounce his newly realized love for the governess, as she recognizes:

> Weil ich dich schon verloren habe, ehe du es ahnst. Weil du mich verlassen mußt. Weil du leben und kämpfen wirst. (P.34)[24]

To be sure, the significance of this relationship takes on a somewhat different color if, as Sachs sees it (probably correctly), the relationship is to be understood as Oedipal.[25] In any case the governess hints at impending disappointment in love and the emptiness of physical love for the emancipated:

> . . . du wirst mir bald sehr wehe tun. Jetzt ist der Stern deines Wagens am höchsten mir zugekehrt, jetzt, wo du noch nichts geliebt und bald alles genossen hast. Diese Stunde kommt nicht wieder. Der Himmel soll dich behüten vor Traurigkeit. (P.32)[26]

The son, after spending the next night with a prostitute who claims to love him and wants to teach him the ways of love, is in fact disappointed:

Im Ernst—sei nicht böse. Ich war enttäuscht. Wie nüch-
tern ist ein Körper und ganz anders, als man sich denkt.
(P.90)[27]

In leaving home he has already renounced his "feeling" in a
confrontation with his father: "Hier endet mein Gefühl"
(p.40).[28]
Nevertheless, from the point of view of the friend he still
basically represents his childhood capacities, not so much
specifically in the power of his love, perhaps, as in his overall
intrinsic vitality. The friend hints at this in explaining why
the son, and not he, must make the crucial speech:

Der Freund. Die Flamme ist mir versagt; . . . Aber du hast
die Gemüter. Ich weiß nicht, wieso, aber du hast sie.
(P.97)[29]

Thus the friend needs him to realize his own ends. He
delivers him from his father's house just in time to interject
him as speaker, under hypnosis, in the grand event prepared
by Cherubim. The friend stands in "counterpoint" (p.61) to
the latter, presumably as Hasenclever's version of the same
basic emancipated type. In a crucial confrontation the friend
forces Cherubim to yield the rostrum and his "greatness,"
tearing the "threads" binding him to von Tuchmeyer (p.79).
In other words, Hasenclever is discarding the Wedekind
model in favor of his own. Telepathically directed by the
friend, the son calls for the abolition of the family as a means
to free oppressed sons. When he demands that fathers be
brought to trial, he is greeted by a storm of enthusiasm from
the audience, followed by alarmed reactions in the news-
papers, suggesting that a new spirit has been released upon
society.
     Controlled by the friend, the son has emancipated himself.
Like Keith he has conquered death and become "immortal"
(p.101). He now closely resembles the friend: "Der Freund.
Nur ein kleiner Raum ist noch zwischen uns beiden—schon
wölbt sich die Brücke des gemeinsamen Stroms" (p.108).[30]
     Where each had been at his own "pole" (p.16), they can
now join at the zenith of a pyramid (p.17). In contrast to

Wedekind's split selves, the friend purposely engineers the transfer of his emancipation to the son and prepares to commit suicide: "Er wird es tun. Triumph! — Hier ist meine Kraft zu Ende" (p.111).[31]

Along with his lack of energy and his emancipation, the friend shows no capacity for love. He ridicules the son's relationship to the prostitute Adrienne and calls the governess a "monster" (p.95). He describes himself as "spoiled in paradise" and "where I flee, alone" (p.16). The friend's final act is to arrange for the son to confront and shoot his father. Despite this willingness to invest his emancipation in the son, this transfer—as previous treatments of the theme would lead us to anticipate—is problematic. He seems to suggest that, in taking his place as the emancipated self, the son will recognize that the friend was part of himself and regret this shift of consciousness:

> Und selbst wenn er die Tat [the murder of the father] begeht, was ist geschehen? Er lebt und wird mich doppelt hassen—wenn der Mantel fällt. (P.111)[32]

This suggests that the son will not integrate the personality, but simply replace him as the emancipated, with nothing gained—at least not from the point of view of an integrated personality.

This pessimistic outlook is only partly and confusingly confirmed in the last act, in which the son, now in full possession of emancipation, confronts the father once more. When the latter refuses to set him free and threatens to have him committed to an asylum, the son aims his revolver at him, whereupon the father dies from a heart attack. In a final lyric exchange with the governess (who now emerges more clearly as a mother-figure), the son summarizes the result of the action. While somewhat confusing, this final passage makes clear that he must leave this new "mother" behind, and that his heart is now empty (p.127). He is

> verschwendet. Vorbei ist nun die große Leidenschaft. Viel ist erfüllt—noch ist mir nichts vollendet; Die Wolke zog dahin. Es blieb die Kraft. (P.127)[33]

The loss of love in emancipation seems clearly expressed: "Ins schmerzlich Ungeliebte, in die Schwere/Des tief Erkannten treibt mein Körper hin" (p.127).[34] Still, a certain vitality has been freed in him: "Jetzt höchste Kraft im Menschen zu verkünden/Zur höchsten Freiheit, ist mein Herz erneut!" (p.128)[35]

It would appear from all this that an integration of the personality was not the goal here. Where emancipation in earlier treatments was regretted as forever cutting the self off from childhood and its promise, for Hasenclever the need for emancipation overrides all other concerns as a primary existential requirement of the self. This one-sided concern betrays a certain shallowness, perhaps an inability to develop the problem in a genuinely dramatic world.

Notes

1. H. MacClean, "Wedekind's *Der Marquis von Keith:* An Interpretation Based on the Faust and Circus Motifs," *Germanic Review* 43 (1968): 164–87.

2. "Wedekind calls his play 'the counterpoint between a Don Quixote of pleasure and a Don Quixote of morality.' This latter, Ernst Scholz, is not only a counterpart to the former, both were born from the poet's dual nature and determined one another. A unity has been analyzed into its extremes, the two souls of one breast" (Artur Kutscher, *Wedekind. Leben und Werk,* ed. Karl Ude [Munich: List Verlag, 1964], p.169).

3. Frank Wedekind, *Der Marquis von Keith,* in *Gesammelte Werke,* vol. 4 [Munich: Georg Müller, 1924], p. 88. All quotations from Wedekind's works will be taken from this edition.

4. "Through real experience you only lose the capacities you brought to the world in your flesh and blood. That applies particularly to you, the son and eventual heir of our greatest German financial genius."

5. "He told me he had originally been a theologian, but lost his faith from too much studying and attempted to find it again the same way the Prodigal Son regained his."

6. "But look, I'm as happy as a person who from earliest childhood has lain in prison and now for the first time in his life is breathing fresh air."

7. "*v.Keith.* My father was as selfless and conscientious as the tutor and educator of a Count Trautenau [Scholz] must be. You were his model child, and I was his whipping boy."

8. "*v.Keith.* My father would turn over in his grave from fright at the thought that you—were asking me for my advice."

9. "Your father contributed a good share to my one-sided intellectual development."

10. "I had changed a railroad regulation. There was a constant danger that this regulation could not possibly be observed precisely. My fears were naturally exagger-

ated, but with each day I saw the catastrophe come closer. I simply lack the psychic balance which a person acquires in a home worthy of a human being.—On the first day after the introduction of my new regulation there was a collision of two express trains that cost nine men, three women and two children their lives."

11. "Naturally I fall dead at the first shot and remain dead until they want to bury me. Only since that day have I felt myself to be the master of my life."

12. *"(Jumping up.)* We do not assume obligations at birth, and one cannot throw away more than this life. He who lives on after death stands above the law."

13. "The Fairy Palace serves me only as a place to collect my energies."

14. "I have behind me a life of ups and downs, but now I'm seriously thinking of building a house; a house with the highest possible ceilings, with a park and an outside staircase. . . . I have finished with the past and do not yearn for it."

15. " . . . then I'll blow the Fairy Palace together with the directorate and stockholders—into the air!"

16. *"Raspe, early twenties, in bright summer dress and straw hat, has the childlike, harmless features of a Guido Reni angel."*

17. "The graves are opening! Sommersberg! And you aren't ashamed to arise from the dead to become secretary of this Fairy Palace?!"

18. *Gesammelte Werke*, vol. 6, p.209.

19. "Do you know that *my* fate resembled *yours,/* That we, although separated through eternities, Have taken the same path, you and I?"

20. Walter Hasenclever, *Der Sohn*. Ein Drama in fünf Akten (Berlin: Propyläen Verlag, 1917), p.74.

21. "It concerns you and me—thus between us alone."

22. Wolfgang Paulsen has seen not Wedekind, but Hofmannsthal (Claudio in *Der Tor und der Tod*) as the model for Hasenclever's use of *Faust* material ("Walter Hasenclever," in *Expressionismus als Literatur. Gesammelte Studien*, ed. Wolfgang Rothe [Bern and Munich: Francke Verlag, 1969], pp. 531 – 47.

23. "This piece was written in the autumn of 1913 and has the purpose of changing the world. It is the presentation of battle through the birth of life. . . . The detour of the offspring to reach its identity; . . . it is the world of the twenty-year-old seen from the soul of the individual. The attempt to embody the counterpoint of the figures in the same actor would clarify the unity of the whole: a spectator who stood at a distance, forgetting the orchestra and stage, would recognize that everything that happens here varies only in the manner of expression of the same idea." Quoted from Miriam Raggam, *Walter Hasenclever. Leben und Werk*. (Hildesheim: Verlag Dr. H. A. Gerstenberg, 1973), p.68.

24. "Because I have already lost you before you realize it. Because you *must* leave me. Because you will live and fight."

25. Hans Sachs, "Der Sohn," *Imago* (1919), pp.43 – 48.

26. "Soon you will hurt me badly. Now your star is in its ascendancy for me, now, when you have not yet loved and soon will have enjoyed everything. This hour will not come again. May heaven protect you from sadness."

27. "Seriously—don't be angry. I was disappointed. How dull a body is, nothing at all like one would expect."

28. "Here ends my feeling."

29. *"The friend.* The flame is denied me; . . . But you have it. I don't know how, but you have it."

30. *"The friend.* Only a small space is still between the two of us—already the bridge of the common flow arches itself."

31. "He'll do it. Triumph!—Here my strength is at an end."

32. "And even if he commits the deed (the murder of the father), what has happened? He will live and hate me twice as much—when the cloak falls."

33. "He is" spent. Past is now the great passion./Much is accomplished—yet nothing is completed;/The cloud drew away. The strength remained."

34. "Into painful lovelessness, into the midst/Of deep recognition does my body carry."

35. "Now to declare highest power in humanity,/The highest freedom, my heart is renewed."

7

Franz Kafka: "Das Urteil"

I

THE split-self theme is central to four of Franz Kafka's most important works: "Das Urteil" (1912), "In der Strafkolonie" (1914), "Ein Landarzt" (1916), and *Das Schloß* (1922). Most of the poets discussed have dropped the theme after a single concentrated treatment, except for echoes in later works. Kafka stands alone, so far, in his extended preoccupation with the theme and his inventiveness in varying the narrative perspective, the symbolic context, and the result of the interaction of the part-selves. Along with stylistic devices derived, as Evelyn Beck has shown, from the Yiddish theater in Prague,[1] the split-self theme provided Kafka with a framework for the characteristic symbolic coherence of much of his work.

While he may have been influenced by Wedekind,[2] neither his own comments nor textual evidence give any real indication of this. The one treatment of the theme known to have had great impact on him and to be reflected motivically in one of his works ("Die Verwandlung"), is Grillparzer's "Der arme Spielmann." Kafka was fascinated by this story and read it several times to his sister.[3] To be sure, "Die Verwandlung" does not contain a split self, except perhaps indirectly in Gregor's ambivalence—outwardly animal and inwardly more human than anyone else would be in his circumstances. But the fact that "Die Verwandlung" and "Das Urteil" were written at about the same time suggests at least that Grillparzer's story was fresh in Kafka's mind when "Das Urteil" was set down. The Kafka criticism has recognized the theme and analyzed the two selves in a variety of ways.[4] To be sure, Albrecht Weber goes too far when he insists that all or none of the main figures of the story must be included in the whole self:

> Der Interpret kann nun, der Schlüssigkeit wegen, das objektiviert Dargestellte wieder ins Innere zurückverlegen und von daher deuten. Dann muß er aber *alle* Figuren des Typengefüges als Kosmos in das Innere zurückverlegen und alle, auch Vater und Braut, als seelische Komponente verstehen. . . . Man kann also nicht, wie White, nur Georg und den Freund als zwei Teile ein und derselben Person ansprechen, den Vater und die Braut aber nicht.[5]

While this universal level is also valid, in a sense, it obscures the more immediate and interpretatively decisive relationship between Georg and the friend. Peter Beicken has summarized a number of the interpretations of the split-self here.[6] Part of his conclusion is particularly interesting in the present context:

> Wie wahre Autonomie und Emanzipation möglich sind, ohne in den negativen Zustand des Freundes zu fallen und ohne die soziale Sphäre verlassen zu müssen, wie also Selbstverwirklichung in der menschlichen Gemeinschaft möglich sei, kommt im "Urteil" kaum in den Blick. (P.250)[7]

The most significant attempt to interpret "Das Urteil"—in fact, Kafka's work in general—from the perspective of two selves is the study of Walter H. Sokel: *Franz Kafka. Tragik und Ironie.*[8] We will examine the story in the light of Sokel's analysis in terms of an "inner" and "outer" self, derived from a passage in Kafka's diary, as well as from the present perspective of oppression versus emancipation. An additional perspective on the problem is afforded by Kafka's initial treatment of the theme in "Die Beschreibung eines Kampfes." It is useful to begin here, as Sokel has done also.

At the beginning of "Die Beschreibung eines Kampfes" (1904/1905) the narrator is sitting at a party apart from the other guests while an "acquaintance" enjoys the attentions of a girlfriend. The narrator deeply resents the fact that this friend possesses love. That the two are parts of one self is first hinted by a comment:

> Mögen sie ihn küssen und drücken, das ist ja ihre Pflicht und sein Recht, aber entführen sollen sie mir ihn nicht. Wenn sie ihn küssen, küssen sie mich ja auch ein wenig, . . . Und er soll immer bei mir bleiben, immer, wer soll ihn beschützen, wenn nicht ich.[9]

The narrator coaxes his friend to leave the confines of the house and embark with him on a walk "in the open" ("im Freien"), where he "obviously became significantly cheerful" (p.13). The implication is that he is in his element in the open and in freedom.

On the way to the Laurenziberg in Prague, the two engage in a subtle battle. The narrator-self first fears that the other will achieve a unification of the personality from *his* point of view and thus destroy him: "Jetzt kam offenbar der Mord. Ich werde bei ihm bleiben" (pp. 21–22).[10]

But the friend proves too weak. He has never been in love prior to his present relationship. Like Keith and Scholz, first the narrator, then the friend falls and injures his knee. The narrator rides on him as on a horse. This suggests a kind of literal unification of the two selves in which the narrator has won out. But it is a Pyrrhic victory and a false synthesis. The injury to the leg of a horse symbolizes mythologically (as we have had occasion to note) something Jung calls the loss of libido.[11] It exactly corresponds to what is happening here. After the two arrive on the Laurenziberg, the friend states that the narrator is incapable of love and has nothing to live for (p.63). However, the narrator suddenly claims to be engaged, thus suggesting that he can in fact love. While he silently congratulates himself for this clever maneuver, the friend, unaware that this is a lie, accepts defeat and commits suicide.

In his diary Kafka described an event in his life in which he sat on a bench on the Laurenziberg—as in the story—and decided that a normal life, and presumably normal love and happiness, were impossible for him. He designated this event as a "Leavetaking . . . from the world of appearances of youth." Strangely, in his account he shifts from the first to the third person, as though to suggest that a change—indeed a loss of—identity took place here.[12]

We see in this early story, then, a conflict between two part-selves, of which one is at first capable of love and the other, while lacking love, feels more at home "in the open." In order to interpret this "original model" of inner conflict, Sokel cites a passage from Kafka's diary, written in 1922:

> Zusammenbruch, Unmöglichkeit zu schlafen, Unmöglich-keit zu wachen, Unmöglichkeit, das Leben, genauer die Aufeinanderfolge des Lebens, zu ertragen. Die Uhren stimmen nicht überein, die innere jagt in einer teuflischen oder dämonischen oder jedenfalls unmenschlichen Art, die äußere geht stockend ihren gewöhnlichen Gang. Was kann anderes geschehen, als daß sich die zwei verschiedenen Welten trennen, und sie trennen sich oder reißen zumin-dest aneinander in einer fürchterlichen Art.[13]

Sokel interprets the two clocks of this passage as the two selves of Kafka's work. The inner, devilish clock represents the same self as the narrator of "Die Beschreibung eines Kampfes," and the external, ordinary clock is the friend, in whom Sokel primarily recognizes a superficial quality, a fa-cade. Sokel's definition of the two selves is difficult to pin down, since he views each as a combination of almost contra-dictory characteristics, emphasizing those the occasion re-quires. The exiled, "eigentliches," pure self is also the devilish self, and the innocent, childlike self is also the "Fassadenmensch" (p.41). He is aware of the problem of loss of the ability to love (p.39), but this remains in the back-ground. While the diary entry is the foundation for his argument, it appears to have created crucial problems for his analysis. The quality of facade, which he sees in the friend in "Die Beschreibung eines Kampfes" and which enables him to make the connection to the diary passage, is not particular-ly applicable to this figure. At best we can speak here of a certain conventionality or normalcy in his love relationship, at most only vaguely commensurate with the diary passage. The later diary entry in fact suggests a totally unrelated principle: the split between the public and the private selves, as described by R.D. Laing.[14] "Die Beschreibung eines Kampfes" makes explicit the fact of a split-self. It also makes explicit and emphatic that the friend is capable of love and that the narrator is not. However it leaves tentative the concept of a balancing advantage of emancipation in the narrator. So far, then, we have argued that Sokel's analysis of the two selves relies upon too heavily and applies too imprecisely a diary passage, written much later. We have suggested an alternative hypothesis based on textual evidence that is only partly complete. Let us treat each view, then, as an hypothesis and see if either makes sense in "Das Urteil."

II

Since a proper representation of Sokel's argument would have to present his words virtually in their entirety, we can only indicate his main thesis here and point to areas of difficulty. As he sees it, Georg Bendemann is the false "Fassadenmensch" whose existence is a denial of the inner, actual self languishing in Russia. Georg's intention to marry is false, based on a fundamental inability to love (p.51). The friend in Russia is the essential self; in fact, in his asceticism he resembles Kafka more than Georg does (p.50). Although this view is internally consistent in many respects and ties in a wealth of details, it results in an untenable devaluation of Georg as opposed to his friend. To be sure, the latter's failure to appear, as well as his passivity and sickliness, can be explained as the effect of Georg's deceit; but Kafka described this friend to Felice Bauer as

. . . kaum eine wirkliche Person, er ist vielleicht eher das, was dem Vater und Georg gemeinsam ist. Die Geschichte ist vielleicht ein Rundgang um Vater und Sohn, und die wechselnde Gestalt des Freundes ist vielleicht der perspektivische Wechsel der Beziehungen zwischen Vater und Sohn.[15]

Georg, then, is the dominant part of the two part-selves. He, alone, dynamically struggles for survival. His destruction at the direction of the father represents a tragic existential failure. But Sokel continues, finding in Georg "... etwas Unschuldiges, Kindliches, und das ist sein bester Teil" (p.55).[16]

And yet, almost in direct contradiction to this, the father is right: each of Georg's actions, superficially thoughtful and fine, turns out to have been devilish and false. Unfortunately, the motif of devilishness that Sokel (agreeing with the father) attributes to Georg contradicts his own definition of the two selves. Georg is supposed to be the facade, while the inner self in Russia is supposed to be the devilish half, according to Sokel's application of the diary passage. This shift of the devilish quality from the friend to Georg further weakens the argument. Sokel appears to be using too freely the motifs suggested in the diary passage. He shifts and combines them in one self or the other, as the occasion requires.

Turning to the concept of oppression versus emancipation, we find that Georg Bendemann claims the ability to love partly in the same way as the acquaintance did in "Die Beschreibung eines Kampfes"; namely, through his engagement. This is consistent with the fact that he has remained in the house of his father; that is, he has not cut himself off from his childhood environment and capabilities. The friend in Russia, on the other hand, has done precisely that—has exiled himself. His sickly constitution and loneliness betray an impoverishment of libido that can be compared to the narrator of "Die Beschreibung eines Kampfes," who could not love. That the friend has insulated himself radically from love can also be seen in his reaction to the death of the person who is in fact his own mother:

> Von dem Todesfall von Georgs Mutter, der vor etwa zwei Jahren erfolgt war und seit welchem Georg mit seinem alten Vater in gemeinsamer Wirtschaft lebte, hatte der Freund wohl noch erfahren und sein Beileid in einem Brief mit einer Trockenheit ausgedrückt, die ihren Grund nur darin haben konnte, daß die Trauer über ein solches Ereignis in der Fremde ganz unvorstellbar wird.[17]

"Das Urteil" is unique among all works that treat this theme (so far as I am aware) in that here the protagonist (with whom the author closely identifies) is still the earlier, gifted self, with salvation in clear view ahead of him. Georg must only attain his independence, which he plans to do by taking over complete responsibility for the business and for his senile father. Thus the friend in Russia will become superfluous and have no existence of his own:

> Das bedeutete aber nichts anderes, als daß man ihm gleichzeitig, je schonender, desto kränkender, sagte, daß seine bisherigen Versuche mißlungen seien, daß er endlich von ihenen ablassen solle, daß er zurückkehren und sich als ein für immer Zurückgekehrter von allen mit großen Augen anstaunen lassen müsse, daß nur seine Freunde etwas verstünden und daß er ein altes Kind sei, das den erfolgreichen, zu Hause gebliebenen Freuden einfach zu folgen habe. (P. 54)[18]

The friend is a separate, competing individual on one level; on another, he represents an element within Georg, who is attempting a delicate and difficult transition from a part-self to a whole self. Thus, when Georg voices his reservations about informing his friend of the engagement, his fiancée suggests with incisive instinct that if Georg has such friends perhaps he should not become engaged at all — that is, if Georg has these inhibitions and cannot love, he should not marry. Georg's paradoxical task requires that he use the independence that his friend affords him as part of him in order to cut himself loose from the friend as representing the inability to love. With one foot in a boat and another on the shore, he hesitates before pushing off through a critical instant when neither the shore nor the boat will be supporting him.

The decisive factor in this delicate situation is the father. Should he show himself weak, dependent, and well-wishing, as at first he seems to do, then Georg is saved. But bringing the matter to the father provides him with a weapon to destroy his son. Before Georg can attain his independence through marriage, the elder Bendemann attacks at the critical, vulnerable moment when Georg is exposing and shedding his emancipated half. First he questions the existence of the friend (logically enough, since the friend is about to cease to exist): "Hast du wirklich diesen Freund in Petersburg?" (p.60).[19] Georg defends himself by pointing out that the friend had once visited and that the father — as one would expect him to react to a son figure who had left the family and rejected the paternal authority — did not particularly like him. When this assault fails, or at least is not overtly successful, the father attacks from a new direction. He contradicts himself by claiming to have secretly corresponded with the friend. Implicitly he is now threatening to support the latter in an attempt to destroy Georg. But this assertion, in contradiction to his earlier position, appears to be a lie, like the narrator's false claim of his engagement in the earlier story. In any case, the attempt to destroy the opponent is successful, and Georg succumbs. The father then proclaims his judgment:

> Jetzt weißt du also, was es noch außer dir gab, bisher wußtest du nur von dir! Ein unschuldiges Kind warst du ja eigentlich, aber noch eigentlicher warst du ein teuflischer Mensch! — Und darum wisse: Ich verurteile dich jetzt zum Tode des Ertrinkens! (P.67)[20]

The first sentence raises the exiled or emancipated self from the verge of extinction to equal status with Georg — in fact greater status, since it enjoys the recognition of the father. The first part of the second sentence suggests, with the use of the past tense, that George, with his childlike innocence, properly belongs to an earlier phase of life, not to the present. The last clause of the sentence condemns Georg — and in the context of the father's attack on his engagement specifically his sexuality, his ability to love — as devilish. Totally overwhelmed, Georg is driven precipitously to carry out the sentence. The moment of fall is accompanied by a final image: "In diesem Augenblick ging über die Brücke ein geradezu unendlicher Verkehr" (p.68).

Kafka explained this in plain language as an ejaculation.[21] At first this appears awkward and best discreetly ignored. But in fact it compresses the entire work into one final image. Just as the friend was on the verge of being destroyed as an independent figure, Georg, through his defeat, has been extinguished as an aspect of personality. This aspect is the ability to love. In a manner masked by banality, the maid labels this sacrifice of love on a religious level by crying out "Jesus," as Georg hurtles past her on his way to the bridge. This use of the Christ symbol might have been inspired by Grillparzer, and in a similar sense: by murdering Christ humanity has turned its back upon the principle of love he represents (cf. also Alfonso's comment in *Die Jüdin von Toledo,* mentioned above). It is the ability to love, also, which, in a purely physical sense, extinguishes itself in the moment of ejaculation. This is Kafka's version of Goethe's "Stirb und werde!"—the image of the moth irresistably drawn to the flame that will consume it.

This image also reflects an element that provides Kafka's treatment of the split self with a peculiar flavor; namely, sexual guilt. With his scorn and ridicule of Georg's love the father has made all sexuality a matter of shame and disgust, of devilishness in his son:

> "Weil sie die Röcke gehoben hat", fing der Vater zu flöten an," weil sie die Röcke so gehoben hat, die widerliche Gans", und er hob, um das darzustellen, sein Hemd so hoch, daß man auf seinem Oberschenkel die Narbe aus seinen Kriegsjahren sah, . . . "Und damit du an ihr ohne Störung dich befriedigen kannst, hast du unserer Mutter Andenken geschändet, den Freund verraten und deinen Vater ins Bett gesteckt." (Pp. 15 – 16)[22]

Despite the father's apparent lies and his dislike of the emancipated self, then, his alliance with the latter has its own logic. Along with its emancipation, this self is also ascetic and has not, therefore, totally overcome the father's influence. Perhaps this is what Kafka had in mind when he said that the friend is what Georg and the father have in common. Thus, Kafka's emancipated protagonists are doomed to remain crippled, damned products of the father. Unlike those of Wedekind, they are ever confronted anew with the threat of the past.

III

In "Das Urteil" Kafka placed the seat of the ego in the earlier figure and demonstrated its demise. Henceforth the childhood self would appear as the other self, promising help or, more often, threatening to drag down the emancipated self, but totally removed from the conscious ego. "In der Strafkolonie" (1914), in this respect, represents a counterpart to "Das Urteil." Here the emancipated self, the "traveling scientist" ("Forschungsreisender"), visits a penal colony, where he is to witness the execution of a prisoner (the earlier self). As a man of science who represents "European" values, the traveler will be decisive in determining the fate of the execution machine, devised by the "old commandant"—a clear father-figure, as he was experienced by the oppressed earlier self. The traveler is honored; his views are respected as those of civilization, just as the emancipated personality finds itself at home in society and in social norms contrasting sharply with the paternal milieu of childhood.

The condemned man has been sentenced to death for having failed to stand on the hour and salute late at night at the door of his superior—a meaningless degradation that conveys the helplessness and rage of the oppressed child. Thus his judgment, which he experiences in the form of words etched by murderous needles on his body, is "honor your superior" or, in psychological terms, "obey the father." As a crushed animal product of the father, the condemned is "animally obedient" (p.98).

It is of interest that the condemned expresses only childhood oppression and not the capability to love. The traveler, conversely, represents only independence, and not a loss of the ability to love. Consequently, the relationship is one-dimensional, and the dramatic tension results not from any vying for domination in synthesis, but from the implicit threat that the traveler might be thrown back together with the condemned. This reflects a threat from the past, perhaps as it exists, as Jung saw it, as present in the unconscious. The traveler remains unaware of this relationship, at least on a conscious level. But subtle hints suggest an unconscious bond between the two part-selves: the traveler's resolve to remain "uninvolved" (p.98), suggesting a need to protect himself; his distraction, as though his conscious mind were beginning to listen in an inward direction (p.100); the condemned man who reaches out toward him, as though to unite them (p.109); the traveler's instinctive backward step from the condemned in the machine (p.111); his reminder to himself that he bears no relationship to the condemned and therefore has no reason to lack objectivity (p.110).

The same terror from childhood threatens the emancipated physician in "Ein Landarzt." He becomes confused in his treatment of the wounded boy (earlier self) and is thrown together with him into the bed. Similarly, the ape in "Ein Bericht für eine Akademie" becomes enraged when it is suggested that, despite his present scholarly activities, he is still basically an ape. He fears that he might fall back through the distant hole through which he came during his process of socialization.

But the old commandant is dead, represented only by the officer, a weakened version of paternal oppression without any power over the traveler. The officer strives to ingratiate himself and frequently smiles in his desperation to have the traveler approve the continued use of the machine. However, beneath all this he still represents the father, repressing rage when he balls his fists (p.116) or when he repeatedly seizes the traveler by the arms, as though to force him (despite all exterior friendliness) to see things his way (pp. 106, 111, 113, 118). At one point, when the traveler fails to show the proper understanding for the machine, the officer considers him a child (p.119).

When, inevitably, the traveler states his final opposition to the machine, the officer releases the condemned and places himself in the machine to be executed, according to the command: "Be just!" The traveler is horrified, first in witnessing the animal revenge of the condemned, then in seeing the machine disintegrate and impale the officer, rather than etch the judgment into his body. Thus the emancipated self, in rejecting the terror of childhood, causes a "revolution" ("grossen Umschwung") (p.122) and assumes the guilt for the destruction of the old paternal order. The guilt feeds on the feeling that the father may have been right, despite his harshness. Just as Georg Bendemann's ability to love was ridiculed and made disgusting by his father's imitation of a girl lifting her skirts, so the officer casts a subtle net of doubt over the values of the traveler and the new commandant. It is the attentions of the "ladies"—what are they doing in a penal colony, anyway?—that raise the questions. They feed sweets to the condemned, who cannot hold them in his stomach. They give him perfumed handkerchiefs, grotesque in the context of his filth. They even—in the imagination of the officer—play with the fingers of the traveler at a decisive public moment, when the fate of the machine is to be decided (p.117).

All of this suggests an unmanly softness and an improper sexuality in the values of the new commandant and the traveler, whose position is undermined. As we have noted, there can be no complete, secure emancipation for Kafka's protagonists. The gravestone of the old commandant reads:

> Es besteht eine Prophezeiung, daß der Kommandant nach einer bestimmten Anzahl von Jahren auferstehen und aus diesem Hause seine Anhänger zur Wiedereroberung der Kolonie führen wird. Glaubet und wartet! (P.126)[23]

"Ein Landarzt" depicts the nightmarish near-loss of emancipation for its title figure, threatened in his professional, emancipated identity by the failure of his diagnosis of the suffering of the earlier self. The boy's suddenly enlarged wound in the side suggests, with its Christian symbolism, that the physician should identify with this suffering and therefore with the boy as part of himself. Instead, like the traveler in "In der Strafkolonie," he flees in panic from the earlier self.

In *Das Schloß* Kafka attempts to bring the emancipated self home to the castle. But the surveyor finds no paternal acceptance. The presumed father figure, Count West-West, is not even mentioned after the beginning; rather, as in the case of the officer, he is replaced by Klamm. The latter is the lowest castle secretary, himself honored as a god by the villagers but buried meaninglessly in endless paper work. The earlier self here is divided into two figures, each representing one major aspect. The oppression is reflected in Barnabas, a spineless, weak-willed individual of no use to the surveyor. His other half, the gifted child, appears in little Hans, through whom the surveyor hopes to gain entrance to the castle. Hans is too young to be of much real help. But at one point he intuits the potential of the surveyor, despite the latter's absurdly low status:

> . . . jetzt sei zwar K. noch niedrig und abschreckend, aber in einer allerdings fast unvorstellbar fernen Zukunft werde er doch alle übertreffen. Und eben diese geradezu törichte Ferne und die stolze Entwicklung, die in sie führen sollte, lockte Hans; . . . .[24]

The surveyor K., as the seat of the ego and a close identification of the author, is driven by the bleakness and nightmarish absurdity of this world to the point of catching a glimpse, through Hans, of his transcendence of it as its Creator. But Kafka permits only a hint of this. The complete realization of such a transcendence of the poetic world would unmask and annihilate it as empty willfulness and throw its author back into his own psychic reality, stripped of his conscious control as Creator. As in "Die Verwandlung" and "Ein Hungerkünstler," the lowly status or demise of the main figure contrasts at great voltage with his tie to the Creator Kafka. It is a role that Kafka can only play, paradoxically, so long as he does not (like Lenz with his Fritz) interfere with the psycho-logic of his Creation.

Notes

1. Evelyn T. Beck, *Kafka and the Yiddish Theater: A Study of the Impact of the Yiddish Theater on the Work of Franz Kafka* (Ph.D. diss., University of Wisconsin, 1970).

2. While Kafka mentions only that he saw Wedekind's *Erdgeist* (where the split self does not occur), his diaries do not cover the relevant years between the appearance of *Keith* and the writing of "Die Beschreibung eines Kampfes" (1904/1905).

3. Heinz Politzer, *Franz Kafka: Der Künstler* (Frankfurt a M: S. Fischer Verlag, 1965), pp.122 – 23.

4. Robert Rogers, for example *(A Psychoanalytic Study of the Double in Literature* [Detroit, Mich.: Wayne State University Press, 1970], pp.51–59) mentions "Das Urteil" as well as "In der Strafkolonie." He sees in the relationship between Georg and his father anal-erotic and sado-masochistic motifs. Where Georg is heterosexual, the friend in Russia is homosexual and totally submissive to the father. Ingo Seidler has argued that a split-self problem (as discussed by Sokel) runs parallel to a religious allegory ("Das Urteil: Freud natürlich? Zum Problem der Multivalenz bei Kafka," in *Psychologie in der Literaturwissenschaft. Viertes Amherster Kolloquium zur modernen deutschen Literatur,* ed. Wolfgang Paulsen [Heidelberg: Lothar Stiehm Verlag, 1971], pp. 174–90). Seidler uses the term "emancipation," but applies it not to the friend, but to Georg: "In Georg selbst möchte ich, im Gegensatz zur gesamten Literatur, das Urbild des emancipierten, dem Glauben seiner Väter untreu und ganz weltlich und materialistisch gewordenen Juden sehen" (p.188). Cyrena N. Pondrom remains close to Sokel's basic concept of Georg as the public facade of the personality, while interpreting the inner self in Russia as the unconscious ("Coherence in Kafka's 'The Judgment': Georg's perceptions of the World," *Studies in Short Fiction* 9 [1972]: 59–79, 65–66).

5. "If he is determined to do so, the critic can return that which is objectively presented back into the inner sphere and interpret it from there. But then he has to return *all* the figures of the structure of character types as a cosmos into the inner sphere and treat all, including father and bride, as psychic components. . . . Thus one cannot, like White, regard only Georg and the friend as parts of one person, but not the father and the bride" (Albrecht Weber, "Das Urteil," in Albrecht Weber, Carsten Schlingmann, and Gert Kleinschmidt, *Interpretationen zu Franz Kafka* [Munich: R. Oldenbourg Verlag, 1968], pp.9–80).

6 Peter U. Beicken, *Franz Kafka: Eine kritische Einführung in die Forschung* (Frankfurt a M: Athenaion Verlag, 1974).

7. "How true autonomy and emancipation are possible without falling into the negative condition of the friend and without having to leave the social sphere—in other words, how self-realization is possible in human society—hardly comes into view in 'Das Urteil.' "

8. Walter Sokel, *Franz Kafka: Tragik und Ironie* (Munich and Vienna: Albert Langen Georg Müller Verlag, 1964), pp.33–43.

9. "Let them kiss and hug him, that is their duty and his right, but they must not alienate him from me. When they kiss him they kiss me a little, too, . . . And he should always remain with me, always, who will protect him if not I? (Franz Kafka, *Die Beschreibung eines Kampfes,* vol. 5 of *Gesammelte Schriften,* ed. Max Brod [New York: Schocken Books, 1946], p.17).

10. "Now, clearly, the murder was coming. I will stay with him."

11. C. G. Jung, *Wandlungen and Symbole der Libido: Beiträge zur Entwicklungsgeschichte des Denkens* 3d ed. (Vienna and Leipzig: Franz Deuticke, 1938), pp. 266,268,269,271,273,398.

12. *Tagebücher 1910–1923,* ed. Max Brod (New York: Schocken Books, 1948/49), p.552. Cf. also Sokel, *op.cit.,* p.41.

13. "Collapse, impossibility to sleep, impossibility to stay awake, impossibility to endure life, more precisely the temporal progression of life. The clocks do not agree, the inner one races in a devilish or demonic or in any case inhuman way, the external one plods along in its usual hesitating walk. What else can happen, but that the two different worlds divide, and they are dividing or at least tearing at one another in a fearsome way" (Sokel, p.41).

14. R. D. Laing, *The Divided Self* (New York: Pantheon Books, 1969).

15. " . . . hardly a real person, he is perhaps more that which the father and Georg have in common. The story is perhaps a circle around father and son, and the

changing figure of the friend is perhaps the change in perspective of the relationship between father and son" (*Briefe an Felice*, ed. Erich Heller and Jürgen Born [Frankfurt a/M: Schocken Verlag, 1967], pp.369–70.

16. " . . . something innocent, childlike, and thaᴛ ıs his best part."

17. "The friend had learned of the death of Georg's mother, which had occurred about two years earlier and since which Georg had lived together with his father. He had expressed his condolences in a letter with a dryness that could only be explained by the fact that the grief over such an event becomes completely unimaginable in a distant land" ("Das Urteil," in *Erzählungen*, 3d ed. [New York: Schocken Books, 1946], p.55). Quotations from Kafka's short stories are taken from this edition.

18. "But that meant nothing less than to say to him at the same time—the more considerately the more injuriously—that his efforts until now had failed, that he should finally give them up, that he must return and let himself be gaped at by everyone, that only his friends knew anything, and that he was an old child that had simply to follow the successful friends that had remained home."

19. "Do you really have this friend in Petersburg?"

20. "Now you know what there was besides you, until now you have known only yourself! You were actually an innocent child, but even more actually you were a devilish person!—And therefore hear: I condemn you now to death by drowning!"

21. Max Brod, *Franz Kafka: Eine Biographie* (Fischer Bücherei, 552; Frankfurt a/M:Fischer Verlag, 1966), p.134.

22. " 'Because she lifted her skirts like this, the disgusting goose,' and, in order to demonstrate this, he lifted his night shirt so high that one saw the scar from his war years on his thigh, . . . 'And in order that you can satisfy yourself with her without being disturbed, you have desecrated the memory of our mother, betrayed your friend and put your father into bed.' "

23. "It is prophesied that after a certain number of years the old commander will be resurrected and lead his followers to reconquer the colony. Believe and wait!"

24. "Now, to be sure, K. was still low and repelling, but in a—to be sure almost inconceivably distant—future time he would surpass everyone. And precisely this absurd distance and the proud development which was supposed to lead into it attracted Hans; . . . " (*Das Schloß* [n.p.: S. Fischer Verlag, 1958], p.152).

8

Hermann Broch:
Die Schlafwandler

I

HERMANN Broch's novel trilogy, *Die Schlafwandler* (1928–1932) presents three slices of modern German history: *1888: Pasenow oder die Romantik; 1903: Esch oder die Anarchie; 1918: Huguenau oder die Sachlichkeit*. Each of these times, as manifested centrally in the title figure, represents a stage in a general "Disintegration of Values," a process of social and religious decline. In Broch's view, this process began with the Reformation (splitting an original Catholic unity into several parts) and reaches a low point in Huguenau's totally value-free, mechanistic existence at the time of Germany's collapse at the end of World War I.

Joachim von Pasenow, central figure of the first novel, represents a conservative, obsolete romanticism, according to the Hegelian definition: "Wenn Irdisches zu Absolutem erhoben wird."[1] In his case, it is expressed by his Prussian lieutenant's uniform and his inhibited, impersonal life style. Pasenow's primary problem is whether and whom to marry and to find the love vaguely lost in his childhood. In the second novel, the accountant August Esch is obsessed with the notion of exacting revenge on a symbol of the great "Accounting Error" in the person of Eduard von Bertrand, a rich homosexual industrialist and a former friend of Joachim von Pasenow. In the third novel, Pasenow and Esch both appear, as town military commandant and newspaper publisher, respectively, but only in tired, empty shells in which the spark of salvation has been extinguished. Similarly, Bertrand, forced by Esch to commit suicide at the end of the second novel, reappears in the superficially unrelated figure of Dr. Bertrand Müller. In this tired and malnourished personality the author Broch makes himself visible just beneath the surface. The central figure of the last novel, Wilhelm Huguenau, is a ruthless scoundrel who murders Esch and emerges unscathed from the collapse of society. All these characters are parts of one self. Specifically, each represents, along with his philosophical role, either the oppressed early self or the emancipated adult. The trilogy thus operates on two main levels: the public level of Broch's theory of values and his epistemology, and the private, personal level of the unconscious, vaguely groping "sleepwalkers" and of the split-self.[2] Broch had this duality of levels in mind when he spoke of the "rational" and the "poetic-irrational":

> Denn jene irrationale Struktur, die dem Dichtergewerbe zugrunde liegt, wird in der ersten Jugend geformt; was nach dem achten Lebensjahr kommt, wird kaum mehr wahrhaft dichterisch-irrational, sondern nur noch rational . . . verarbeitet.[3]

Broch's own method is characterized by a highly conscious, hence rational manipulation of motifs, each a nugget of given, unreflected, irrational reality. The resulting world is essentially Broch's own conscious construction, a matrix of motifs in which virtually nothing remains as merely naturalistic detail, but is locked into a complex structure of relationships.

Like most of his predecessors in the treatment of the split self, Broch implanted evidence of his sources in the text. The more obvious is Goethe. The emancipated Bertrand is called a "Mephisto"; indeed, before he actually appears, after his return from a trip to America, he is fearfully awaited by Joachim, who needs his protection from his father during the latter's visit with him in Berlin; in fact, Joachim conjures him up—or attempts to do so. In a letter to Herbert Bergmüller, Broch expressed his recognition of this theme in Goethe's life and the problem of creating a new synthesis of the part-selves:

> Und da will mir nun scheinen, daß Sie sich in einer höchst bedenklichen Spaltung befinden, in einer Auseinander-reißung des Verstandesmäßigen, des Gefühlsmäßigen, des Triebmäßigen, in einer inneren Personszersplitterung, die zwar für den Dichter wahrscheinlich unerläßlich ist, da er sonst niemals dramatisch denken könnte—auch Goethes Leben war ein spezifisch aufgespaltenes—, die aber gleich-zeitig seine höchste Gefahr ist; denn das Kunstwerk, die Dichtung, gelingt nur, wenn es dem Dichter gelingt, im Werk seine Person wieder zu sammeln und zur Einheit zu bringen, wofür wieder Goethe als Beispiel anzuführen ist.[4]

Broch's other source for the split-self was Kafka. Evidence for this in the text is just adequate to make this connection a strong likelihood. A number of motifs point specifically to "Das Urteil." Pasenow, like Georg Bendemann, inwardly struggles with the impediments to marriage, which he be-lieves will go against or destroy an emancipated friend (Ber-trand) and the father. Thus Pasenow is convinced, when he announces his engagement to Elisabeth, daughter of neighboring landed gentry, that this move will destroy Ber-trand and his father:

> Der Gedanke verließ ihn nicht und am nächsten Morgen steigerte er sich sogar zu einer Art Gewißheit, und wenn schon nicht zu einer Gewißheit des Todes, so doch der Nicht-Existenz: der Vater und Bertrand waren aus diesem Leben geschieden, und wenn er auch selber an solchem Tode mitschuldtragend war, so blieb doch alles in geruh-samer Gleichgültigkeit, und er mußte nicht einmal mehr darüber nachdenken, ob es Elisabeth oder Ruzena war, die er jenem geraubt hatte. (Pp.153–54)[5]

Like the old Bendemann, Joachim's father questions the role of the emancipated Bertrand, whereby the use of the word "Schadenfreude" exemplifies the finely spun and subtle play on a source:

Er ließ es hingehen, daß der Vater seine Briefschaften durch-
stöberte und wenn sie ihm dann mit den Worten überge-
ben wurden: "Scheint leider noch immer keine Nachricht
von deinem Freund dabei zu sein; ob er nur überhaupt
kommt", so wollte Joachim, trotzdem es ihm wie Schadenfreude klang, bloß das Bedauern heraushören. (P.79)[6]

Just as the elder Bendemann claimed correspondence with
the friend as a weapon against Georg, the elder Pasenow
examines the mail. When Bertrand does arrive, he secretly
offers to accept him and disinherit Joachim (p.96).

Where Georg's fiancée sensed the problem of "such
friends," Joachim's girl friend, the *Animiermädchen* Ruzena—
whom he, in his inhibition, passes over for the more respect-
able but uninteresting Elisabeth—recognizes in Bertrand
(and interprets Kafka's phrase as) the "bad friend" (e.g.,
p.82). She senses that he is responsible for Joachim's turning
away from her, even though Bertrand has done nothing
against her. In fact, as is inherent specifically in Kafka's
development of the emancipated self, Bertrand represents in
his very existence a principle of asceticism (and not, for
example, a jaded indulgence), the element within Joachim
that will destroy his love and with it the only chance for
salvation in the trilogy. Although outwardly he agrees with
Ruzena in order to calm her down, even Bertrand admits his
function: "Ruzena, ich bin doch schlechter Mensch und dein
Feind" (p.83).[7]

Otherwise Bertrand is compared to a "Forschungsreisender"—a somewhat unusual term not likely to be accidental
here, particularly in a context that includes the fact that he is
admired expressly by "ladies" (p.93)—just as in Kafka's "In
der Strafkolonie."

This evidence, subtly assimilated into the text, along with
Broch's development of the split-self theme, designates
Kafka in all likelihood as Broch's primary source for the
problem; moreover, it accounts for the general situation and
Problemstellung in the first novel of the trilogy.

II

More like Lenz or Schiller than Kafka, however, Broch splits the self into three stages. The first is Helmuth, who never actually appears but is killed in a duel early in the novel. The father keeps insisting that he fell "for the honor of the name" (p.42)—perhaps over rumors of the old Pasenow's relations with the Polish maids at the estate. But this, in keeping with Broch's practice of smearing the outer edges of his motif systems into the organic and indeterminate, is never made clear. In any case Helmuth is felt to be destroyed, both directly and indirectly, by the father, and in a manner suggestive of the old Bendemann:

> Nichtsdestoweniger erhielt sich hartnäckig das Gerücht, daß der Alte durch irgendwelche Machinationen mit der Post eine Heirat und das Glück seines Sohnes zerstört habe. (P.67)[8]

As the oppressed son Helmuth also—in a conservative, conventional way—inwardly embodies a healthier, more unified system of values than Joachim (p.41). Bertrand is at the opposite pole. Where Helmuth as first-born son had to remain home while Joachim was sent to military school, Bertrand also attended the school at the same time, but we learn nothing about his life prior to this. Where Joachim hated the school and wanted to return home, Bertrand left the school for a more emancipated civilian life. Thus all three figures are closely tied, one essentially without an adulthood, one without a childhood, and one caught in the middle.

As the central figure of the first novel Joachim is dynamically suspended between Helmuth and Bertrand. He gropes vaguely in intellectual darkness for a clear system of values to live by. He is attracted to Ruzena but feels threatened by her in his conservatism. He conjures up Bertrand both as emancipation-protection from the father and as inhibition-protection from Ruzena. But Bertrand does not appear when called forth, suggesting his independence from Joachim (p.17). Indeed Joachim, although the central figure here and the focus of the narrative perspective, is not the seat of the ego in the split self. It is Bertrand whom Broch described as the secret "main figure" of the trilogy.[9] Therefore when Joachim at the end of the first novel believes he is destroying Bertrand, it is he, and not Bertrand, who will be absent from the second part. Joachim is too weak and confused either to destroy Bertrand or to assume (like Hasenclever's "son") his emancipation. He is locked into the misery of an "in-between," possessing neither Bertrand's complete intellectual freedom nor Helmuth's conservative values. His existential destruction is well expressed in Part IV of the first novel:

> Nichtsdestoweniger hatten sie nach etwa achtzehn Monaten ihr erstes Kind. Es geschah eben. Wie sich dies zugetragen hat, muß nicht mehr erzählt werden. Nach den gelieferten Materialien zum Charakteraufbau kann sich der Leser dies auch allein ausdenken. (P.170)[10]

The text is full of passages playing upon the identity of these three figures:

> Der Pastor trat ein und Bertrand wurde als Freund Joachims vorgestellt. "Ja, der eine kommt, der andere geht", meinte Herr v. Pasenow sinnend, und die Anwesenden wußten nicht, ob diese Anspielung auf den armen Helmuth eine Freundlichkeit oder eine Grobheit für Bertrand bedeuten sollte. (P.89)[11]

The split self is tied clearly to the philosophical level:

> "Wir sind anders als er", erwiderte sie. Joachim war gerührt, daß sie "wir" gesagt hatte. "Er ist vielleicht entwurzelt," sagte er, "und vielleicht sehnt er sich zurück." Elisabeth sagte: "Jeder ist in sich beschlossen." "—Doch haben wir nicht das bessere Teil behalten?" fragte Joachim. . . . "denn er lebt für Geschäfte und er muß kalt und gefühllos sein. Denken Sie doch an Ihre Eltern, an die Worte Ihres Herrn Vaters. Er aber nennt es Konvention; ihm fehlt die wahre Innigkeit und Christlichkeit." Er verstummte: ach, das Gesagte, es war ja nicht echt gewesen. (P.150)[12]

A good example of the concentration with which the split self
dominates much of the text is found on page 52. Bertrand is
supposed to have met Helmuth, but with his "amazing
memory" Broch hints of a deeper-seated relationship. Bertrand fixes Helmuth in time as a boy: "Ja, er war ein blonder,
stiller Junge, sehr verschlossen . . . er dürfte sich auch später
nicht viel verändert haben."[13] From his perspective Helmuth
and Joachim must both appear as oppressed: " . . . übrigens
war er Ihnen ähnlich."[14] This idea threatens Joachim, who
fears that Bertrand is attempting to destroy him with this
identification: "Das war nun wieder etwas zu vertraulich, fast
schien es, als wollte Bertrand den Tod Helmuths für sich
ausnützen."[15]

In defense, Joachim somewhat maliciously interprets Bertrand's memory of his military school years as an indication of
his desire to return to childhood; i.e., in the direction of
Joachim's identity:

> . . . übrigens war es kein Wunder, daß Bertrand sich aller
> Begebenheiten seiner einstigen militärischen Karriere so
> erstaunlich genau entsann; man erinnert sich gerne
> glänzenderer Zeiten, deren man verlustig geworden ist.[16]

These passages must serve merely as examples of the
wealth of split-self motifs extending throughout the trilogy
and generating ever new aspects of the theme to be developed.

III

Like Schiller and Wedekind, Broch provides an event that
represents the actual split in the self. This is the "Ponyaffaire" in which Joachim, shortly before being sent off to
military school, rides on muddy ground the horse belonging
jointly to Helmuth and himself. As a result, the horse breaks
its leg:

> Diese Wochen waren eine unheilschwangere und doch
> eine gute Zeit; niemals, weder früher noch später, war er

mit dem Bruder so befreundet gewesen. Dann allerdings
kam das Unglück mit dem Pony. . . . es bestand ein
strenges Verbot, bei solchem Boden auf die Felder zu
reiten. Joachim aber fühlte das bessere Recht des Scheid-
enden, . . . Nur zu einem ganz kurzen Galopp hatte er
angesetzt, als schon das Unglück geschehen war; der Pony
geriet mit dem Vorderbein in eine tiefe Grube, überschlug
sich und konnte nicht mehr aufstehen. . . . Joachim sah
noch, wie er und Helmuth dort knieten und den Kopf des
Tieres streichelten, aber er vermochte sich nicht mehr zu
entsinnen, wie sie heimgekommen waren, . . . Dann hatte
er die Stimme der Mutter gehört: "Man muß es Vater
sagen." . . . Endlich klemmte der Vater das Einglas ins
Auge: "Es ist die höchste Zeit, daß du aus dem Hause
kommst," . . . Dann sah er noch, wie der Vater die Pistole
aus dem Kasten nahm. Ja, und dann erbrach er sich. Am
nächsten Morgen erfuhr er von dem Arzte, daß er eine
Gehirnerschütterung erlitten hätte, . . . es war wieder eine
gute Zeit, sonderbar geborgen und abgerückt von allen
Menschen. Trotzdem nahm sie ein Ende und mit einer
Verspätung von einigen Wochen wurde er nach Culm in die
Anstalt eingeliefert. . . . da schien es fast, als hätte er jene
Abgerücktheit mit herübergenommen, und dies machte
ihm den Aufenthalt fürs erste erträglich. (Pp. 12 – 13)[17]

This superficially harmless and not particularly impressive
passage is the triumph of Broch's synthetic method. Not only
the split-self, but major Freudian and Jungian themes, along
with a number of offshoot motifs, intersect and unite here. An
impetus of synthesis and motif interaction is generated here
and carries not only throughout the trilogy, but also centrally
into Broch's later novel, *Der Tod des Vergil.* In his essay,
Hofmannsthal und seine Zeit, Broch expressed the function of
the symbol in terms clearly applicable to this passage:

. . . nicht Symbolfülle ist das Charakteristikum der monu-
mentalen Kunst, sondern das Essentialsymbol ist es, das
Symbol, das in einem einzigen Bild, in einem einzigen
Geschehen das Schicksal einer Gesamtheit und sohin auch
das all ihrer Glieder erfaßt und zusammenfaßt.[18]

The Jungian or mythological level—it is not clear through
what specific sources Broch developed this motif[19]—empha-

sizes the horse's broken leg as the loss of libido. This signals the loss of childhood capabilities and the onset of emancipation:

> Oben sahen wir, daß die Libido zur Mutter geopfert werden mußte, um die Welt zu erzeugen, hier wird die Welt aufgehoben durch die erneute Opferung derselben Libido, die erstmals der Mutter gehörte. Das Pferd kann daher füglich als Symbol für diese Libido eingesetzt werden, indem es, wie wir sahen, vielfache Beziehung zur Mutter hat. Durch die Opferung des Roßes kann also nur wieder ein Introversionszustand erzeugt werden, der dem vor der Weltschöpfung gleicht.[20]

This cosmic introversion is echoed in Joachim's "Abrückung," which results from the accident and by means of which he protects himself from loneliness at the military school. The sacrifice of the horse also represents a sacrifice of the "universe," commensurate with its unifying and central role in Broch's work:

> Wie Deussen bemerkt, hat das Roßopfer die Bedeutung einer Entsagung auf das Weltall. Wenn das Roß geopfert wird, so wird gewissermassen die Welt geopfert und zerstört.[21]

The three-legged horse, resulting in effect from the "Ponyaffaire," also functions in a manner connecting this libido problem with the devil or Mephisto:

> Noch einer Symbolform ist zu gedenken: Gelegentlich reitet der Teufel auf einem dreibeinigen Pferd. Die Todesgöttin Hel reitet in der Pestzeit ebenfalls auf einem dreibeinigen Pferd.[22]

The three-legged horse plays an explicit role in the novel even before the "Ponyaffaire," at the very beginning of the trilogy. Here some hypothetical "young person blinded by hatred" (obviously the son) would like to destroy the irritating gait of the old Pasenow:

. . . um dem, der so geht, einen Stock zwischen die Beine
zu stecken, ihn irgendwie zu Fall zu bringen, ihm die
Beine zu brechen, solche Gangart für immer zu vernichten.
(P.8)[23]

Already three-legged by virtue of his cane, the old Pasenow is
seen as a horse, and is also connected with the devil:

> So gehen Beine und Stock nebeneinander, und nun taucht
> die Vorstellung auf, daß der Mann, wäre er als Pferd zur
> Welt gekommen, ein Paßgänger geworden wäre; aber das
> Schrecklichste und Abscheulichste daran ist, daß es ein
> dreibeiniger Paßgang ist, . . . daß so der Teufel schlendert,
> ein Hund, der auf drei Beinen hinkt. (Pp. 8–9).[24]

This motivic prefiguration of the "Ponyaffaire" is meaningful
only retroactively, as a subtle, unconscious preparation for the
key event; or, as Broch conceptualized it, in the sense of the
musical simultaneity of a symphony.

The "Ponyaffaire" also contains an important Freudian
motif. Freud was a source of a number of motifs for Broch
(e.g., Bertrand's "wegwerfende Handbewegung" and the
title of the trilogy itself), as well as philosophical and psychological questions that found expression in Broch's works. But
for the "Ponyaffaire" Broch borrowed specifically from
Freud's "Analyse der Phobie eines fünfjährigen Knaben." A
troubled and disturbed boy, Oedipally tied to his mother
(who insisted on keeping him in bed with her), desired the
destruction of his father. He displaced this censored desire
upon horses, which he unconsciously identified with the father. The implication is that he wished the horse would fall
and break its leg (as at the beginning of the novel and in the
"Ponyaffaire").[25] While in major respects unrelated to the
mythological significance of the horse and raising no claims to
general archetypal significance, this psychoanalytic source
provides Broch with the means to complete a three-way interlocking system of motifs. The Freudian Oedipal theme here
identifies the destruction of the horse with the destruction of
the father. This motif is also indirectly expressed in Joachim's
guilt feelings toward Helmuth, who as an earlier self (left

behind after the "Ponyaffaire") obeyed the father and manifested the latter's values.

The Freudian Oedipal theme (in its application to a specifc
case that involves the horse as a symbol of the father) thus
unites the act of emancipation central to the split-self (as
derived from Kafka and Goethe) with the Jungian loss of
libido and the mythological significance of the horse.

The final source of malaise, then (on the psychological
level) is the Oedipal problem—a theme that emerges more
openly and explicitly in Huguenau's assault on Esch's wife,
"Mother" Hentjen, as well as in Esch's choice of such a figure
in marriage. The expression of these impulses is also meaningful on the philosophical level, as a specific result of the
deterioration of cultural values. Joachim's conscious attitude
toward his mother—object of his final, deepest inhibition—is
characterized by the active repression of his true emotions and
by the resentment of a person who "was in league with a
common enemy [the father]" (p.10). It is no accident that all
of this material appears to be dominated by a childhood
trauma, such as emphasized in early psychoanalysis as the key
to later neuroses. Broch pointed out that it was his psychoanalysis with a Dr. Schaxel that inspired him to write *Die
Schlafwandler*.[26]

IV

The pessimism and hopelessness of a therapy focusing thus
on the past and insisting (in all probability) on the universal
importance of Oedipal problems avenge themselves magnifi-
cently in the text as the motifs expand and abstract themselves outward through the trilogy. Such motifs as the cane,
limping, the return home, the caressing of the head, and so
on, derive their initial meaning from the "Ponyaffaire." But
the central, unifying motif in the sense of the Hofmannsthal
essay remains the horse. Joachim stages another "Ponyaffaire" after Helmuth's death, when he first tries to get Bertrand's horse to fall; then, when this fails, he forces his own
horse to stumble and claims that it is badly injured. Both

efforts represent the attempt to sacrifice emancipation in favor of Helmuth.

Another example is provided by the senile town commandant in the third novel. Joachim is injured in a car accident during the Revolution, and in his dying delirium he imagines that his horse has broken its leg. Thus he inwardly recreates and re-experiences the "Ponyaffaire" in his final moments. The horse itself is abstracted from this incident—first into other horses, where one notices specifically the leg:

> Das Weinlaub an den Zäunen der Vorgärten war rot, . . . und die Pferde vor den vier Droschken an der Strassenecke drüben hatten traurig und friedlich gebeugte Vorderbeine. (P.116)[27]

At the end, horses (needed for the war effort) are noticeably absent: " . . . da ist das Kind in ein unbekanntes Dorf gelangt, stolpert durch stumme Gassen, in denen hie und da ein Fuhrwerk ohne Gespann steht" (P.63).[28]

August Esch gradually assumes horse-like qualities:

> Esch hörte ihm nicht zu, sondern ging mürrischvergrämten Gesichts im Zimmer auf und ab, mit schweren ungelenken Schritten die schlecht zu seiner Hagerkeit paßten. Der gescheuerte Fußboden knarrte unter dem schweren Tritt, und Huguenau betrachtete die Löcher und den Mauerschutt zwischen den Dielen, sowie Herrn Eschs schwere schwarze Halbschuhe, die merkwürdig nicht mit Schuhbändern, sondern mit einer an Sattelzeug gemahnenden Schnalle verschlossen waren. (P.384)[29]

This horse characteristic infuriates Huguenau—he doesn't know why—and motivates the murder of Esch (p.650). But Huguenau himself has been infected by Esch's sarcastic horse grin. The motif finally ends in a distant unification with that of Bertrand's ironic grin in Huguenau's descendants:

> . . . daß sich da bei einem von ihnen ein sarkastisch-ironischer Zug ausprägen werde, war nicht zu vermuten gewesen. Doch ob dies in der Mischung des Blutes bedingt oder bloßes Spiel der Natur war oder etwas, das eine Vollendung

des Enkels zeigt und ihn von allen seinen Ahnen löst, ist
schwierig zu entscheiden und ein Detail, auf das niemand,
am allerwenigsten Huguenau selber, irgendeinen Wert
legt. (P.669)[30]

Other motifs, related to the horse through the "Ponyaffaire," carry in other directions; for example, the cane and
limping, as they occur in various figures in the trilogy.
The two part-selves, similarly, are abstracted into the figures of the second and third novels. While Bertrand, contrary
to Joachim's expectations, survives into the second period
(1903), Joachim is replaced there by Esch, a Joachim born a
generation later in an anarchy of values. As an intensified
version of the earlier figure, Esch, an orphan, "hardly" knew
his mother, for example, where Joachim's relationship to his
mother was merely inhibited. As an "Erbderivat" of Joachim
(to use Broch's term for Huguenau in relation to Bertrand),[31]
Esch cannot find any direct thread leading to a problem and a
solution directly applicable only to Joachim. He can only
abstract his vague, intuitive "sleepwalking" awareness of loss
of salvation into a great "Accounting Error" and note the
principle of transference from one person to another:

Irgendwo kam es eben nicht mehr auf die Menschen an,
die waren alle gleich und es verschlug nichts, wenn einer
im andern verfloß und der eine auf dem Platz des andern
saß. (P.257)[32]

One of Esch's functions is to avenge the existential destruction of Joachim. He does this in a most appropriate manner,
despite the fact that he has no connection to Joachim at all on
a realistic level: he singles out Bertrand as the Evil One and
attacks him specifically for his sacrifice of love; i.e., his
homosexuality. Exposed, Bertrand obliges him by commit-
ting suicide. Esch's unerring, if unconscious, intuition even
rises to the surface in an observation applicable only to Joachim. Esch resents his role as avenger:

" . . . die Toten waren auch anständig, freilich, wie es um
diese Anständigkeit bestellt ist, das sieht man an der Erb-
schaft, die sie einem hinterlassen haben." "Was heißt das?"

Esch zuckte die Achsel: "Nichts, ich meinte bloß so."
(P.312)[33]

Even this abstraction of selves across a gulf of time and place
appears to be paralleled in the mythological meaning of the
horse:

> Wenn das Epos Parikshits Geburt und Erweckung mit der
> Feier des Pferdeopfers in Verbindung bringt, so geschieht
> dies in der Absicht, Zeiten und Männer, die ein weiter
> Zwischenraum trennt, in unmittelbaren Zusammenhang zu
> bringen.[34]

Just as Pasenow, eliminated at the end of the first novel, is
replaced by Esch, so Bertrand, eliminated by Esch's discovery of his homosexuality, is replaced in the third novel by the
unscrupulous, radically emancipated Huguenau, murderer of
Esch.
But Bertrand is replaced also by the contrastingly positive
(if more passive) Dr. Bertrand Muller. That this figure is
meant to represent the author Broch entering his poetic world
is suggested for example by his vain attempts to unite the
young Jew Nuchem with the Christian Salvation Army girl
Marie:

> Denn selbst Nuchem und Marie sind mir fremd, sie, denen
> meine letzte Hoffnung gegolten hat, die Hoffnung, daß ich
> ihr Schicksal in die Hand genommen hätte, es zu bestim-
> men. Nuchem und Marie, sie sind nicht meine Geschöpfe
> und waren es niemals. Trügerische Hoffnung, die Welt
> formen zu dürfen! (Pp.590–91)[35]

With Bertrand Müller's emergence as author-creator, his substance within the world of the novel thus threatens to dissolve
into a transcendental transparency, and his puppets threaten
to come to a halt:

> Die beiden aber standen nun da mit hängenden Armen,
> getrauten sich nicht, einander anzufassen, nicht zu tanzen,
> mit blödem Lächeln standen sie da. (P.527)[36]

Bertrand Müller summarizes his endeavor as the search for a unity of self (cf. Broch's letter to Bergmüller quoted above):

> Ich bin viele Wege gegangen, um den Einen zu finden, in dem alle anderen münden, indes sie führten immer weiter auseinander, und selbst Gott war nicht von mir bestimmt, sondern von den Vätern. (P.592)[37]

He draws a final balance:

> Ich sagte zu mir: "Du bist ein Trottel, du bist ein Platoniker, du glaubst, die Welt erfassend, sie dir gestalten zu können und dich selbst zu Gott zu erlösen. Merkst du nicht, daß du daran verblutest? (P.592)[38]

V

Both the split-self and the related symbol of the horse[39] figure prominently in Broch's later novel, *Der Tod des Vergil* (1945). Famous for its long, lyrically abstract sentences of interior monologue, this Joycean work portrays the last day in Virgil's life: the landing in Augustus's retinue at Brundisium; the passage of the dying poet through the crowded streets to the palace; and the final hours of feverish fantasy and self-doubt, interrupted by a discussion with Augustus, who wants the *Aneid*, which Virgil has planned to burn.

Seen against the backdrop of *Die Schlafwandler*, *Der Tod des Vergil* appears as a massive new effort to gather up the abstracted, outward-expanding, hopeless motifs of the earlier work and turn them backward and inward toward a mystical center. This is achieved in part by substituting for the viewpoint of psychoanalysis a more mystical Jungian glimpse of the self returning to the All in a reversal of Creation.

The emancipated self is Virgil, who is facing death and looking back upon a life without meaning or fulfillment. The counterfigure is the boy Lysanias, who appears from nowhere to lead Virgil and his bearers through the hostile crowd to the palace. He remains there, half real, half product of delirium, in the feverish inner experience of the dying poet. Lysanias is

the positive child-genius, like Kafka's Hans. Broch claimed to
have conceived this figure spontaneously in a trance-like
state. He may also have been influenced by his reading and
then forgotten his source.[40] Either way, Lysanias's function
closely coincides with a number of characteristics of the
mythological child-figure as presented in a study by Jung and
Karl Kerényi, *Das göttliche Kind*.[41] Here a mythological pattern
of the child as *Führergestalt* is analyzed as bearing the life-
promise lost from the adult personality. (This brings us back
to the Jungian observations mentioned in the first chapter of
this study). Thus Lysanias informs Virgil: "Immer hast du
dich gesucht, um mich zu finden, und dich findend hast du
mich gesucht."[42]

Like the child-figure as discussed by Jung and Kerényi,
Lysanias is both godlike and helpless. At one moment he
leads Virgil with his torch and, at the next, obliviously and
banally plays with other children:

. . . verlöscht und kaltverkohlt war der Fackelstumpf in
seinen Händen—balgte er sich lustig mit den anderen, als
gäbe es nichts auf der Welt außer solchem Spiel . . . Und
siehe da, der Lysanias gab überhaupt keine Antwort mehr;
als hätte er einen Fremden vor sich, schaute er nur ganz
flüchtig herauf, um unverzüglich sich wieder seinem Spiel
zuzuwenden. (P.463)[43]

This corresponds to Jung's comment:

Es ist ein auffallendes Paradoxon in allen Kindesmythen,
daß einerseits das "Kind" übermächtigen Feinden ohn-
mächtig ausgeliefert und von beständiger Auslöschungs-
gefahr bedroht ist, andererseits aber über Kräfte verfügt,
welche menschliches Maß weit übersteigen. Diese Aussage
hängt eng zusammen mit der psychologischen Tatsache,
daß das "Kind" einerseits zwar "unansehnlich", d.h. uner-
kannt, "nur ein Kind", andererseits aber göttlich ist.[44]

The primary duality of Virgil and Lysanias is widened into
a Jungian unity of total personality, based on the number
four. Thus the slave, a shadowy figure, lurks disturbingly in

the background of Virgil's fantasy and vaguely represents the
father through the motifs of the cane and of limping. Virgil's
mistress Plotia, also only indirectly involved through his
fantasy, joins in this unity:

> . . . erkannte er den Lysanias in der Plotia, und der Lysa-
> nias war er selber, erkannte er den Sklaven in dem Lysa-
> nias, und der Sklave war er selber. (Pp. 512– 13)[45]

Aniela Jaffe has supplied the Jungian explanation:

> In dieser Coniunctio entsteht eine hermaphroditische
> Lichtgestalt, welche jedoch bald ihre Ergänzung in der
> Gestalt des Sklaven und in derjenigen der Ichpersönlich-
> keit des Dichters findet. Erst in dieser vierfachen Einheit
> entsteht die Ganzheit des Menschen, welche Bewußtsein
> und Unbewußtes umfaßt.[46]

This (perhaps a bit facile) synthesis is only a momentary stage
in Virgil's process of unification with ever widening circles:
humanity, animal life, the universe. The entire process suggests more a dissolution of self than a new unity of personality.

Before a return to cosmic origins can take place, Virgil
questions whether any alternative to his fearful progress
toward death might have been possible for him; whether any
other path in life might have been available. The answer
comes in the form of three figures that appear in the night
below his palace window: a father (identified among other
things by the *Schlafwandler* motifs of limping and cane), a
woman, and a large man with "child-hands"—hence a son
who had remained in the family rather than emancipate himself. Appearing momentarily out of the darkness in the dimly-
lit street, they argue violently. The child-man then mounts an
Oedipal assault on the mother and is struck down by the
father:

> . . . denn der Dickwanst. . . . trachtete, . . . lüstern bittend
> die Hände vorgestreckt, an die schimpfend und fluchend
> zurückweichende Frau heranzugelangen, . . . taubblind
> auf sein Ziel gerichtet und sicherlich nicht gewillt davon

abzulassen, hätte nicht ein überraschender Stockhieb des leise Herbeigehinkten dem Spiel plötzlich ein Ende bereitet: . . . der Dicke war einfach hingeplumpst, wälzte sich ein wenig und blieb dann ruhig liegen—, der Mörder jedoch scherte sich nicht weiter um ihn (pp. 124–25).[47]

Broch's final image of this alternate self points to Kafka's "Verwandlung":

. . . da regte sich der Gefallene, und nachdem er es zustande gebracht hatte, sich in die Bauchlage zu drehen, krabbelte er auf allen vieren wie ein Tier, wie ein großer plumper Käfer . . . eilends den Gefährten nach. Nicht Komik, nein, Schrecknis und Furchtbarkeit umwitterten das Fabeltier. (Pp. 125–26)[48]

This revolting alternative of an emancipation not undertaken, of an oppressed son sexually tied to his mother, thus plays itself out before Virgil's eyes. It helps to demonstrate that his life of emancipation was the only choice for him.

In *Die Schlafwandler* the half-oppressed, half-emancipated figures of Pasenow and Esch failed to seize the salvation in love available in Ruzena and Ilona, respectively. For both, emancipation meant a sleepwalking confusion of exile from their origins and from a yearned-for social order. The emancipated figures of Bertrand and Huguenau, both consciously adequate to deal with a disintegrating society, left irretrievably behind them the salvation in love available to Pasenow and Esch. In *Der Tod des Vergil*, like Kafka in *Das Schloß*, Broch splits the earlier self into the godlike child and a purely negative oppressed son (the "beetle" of the night scene) beaten down by the father. Here the emancipated Virgil, after reviewing with despair an empty life, finds a mystical exit from the problem— a solution that eluded Wedekind, for example. Here Broch brings the split-self to its ultimate resolution, having developed it from the sources of Goethe and Kafka through the synthesis with Freudian and Jungian material to a lyric-mystical dissolution in the cosmos. No one took the problem more seriously than Broch, and no one strove more intensely than he to make poetry a means to deal with reality.[49]

Notes

1. "When worldly things are raised to the absolute" (Hermann Broch, *Die Schlaf-wandler*, vol. 2 of *Gesammelte Werke*, 10 vols. [Zurich: Rhein-Verlag, 1953–61], p.19). All quotations from Broch's works are taken from this edition. For a more detailed treatment of much of the material of this chapter see my *Die Kindheitsproblematik bei Hermann Broch* (Munich: Wilhelm Fink Verlag, 1968).

2. The claim that the split-self theme is central to the trilogy must contend with other perspectives which have been offered as unifying the novel, such as Broch's theory of values, his epistemology, or the symbolism of the Apocalypse.' (For the last, see Heinz D. Osterle, *"Die Schlafwandler:* Revolution und Apocalypse," *PMLA* 86 (5) [October, 1971]; 946–58). While all of these approaches cannot be of equal importance, the point is that Broch strove to integrate the work not only horizontally in his texture of motifs, but vertically through several levels of meaning.

3. "For that irrational structure which is the foundation for the trade of the poet is formed in earliest childhood; what comes after the age of eight is hardly assimilated in a truly poetic-irrational way any longer, but only rationally" (*Briefe* [*Gesammelte Werke*, vol. 8], p.404).

4. "And there it seems to me that you find yourself in a most dubious split, in a tearing apart of reason, emotion, drives, in an inner splitting of personality which, to be sure, is probably necessary for the poet, since otherwise he could never think dramatically. Goethe's life, too, was specifically split. But this is at the same time the poet's greatest danger; for the work of art, poetry, is successful only when the poet succeeds in collecting his self again in his work and bringing it to a unity, for which Goethe again is a good example" (Ibid., p.134).

5. "The thought did not let him alone and the next morning it intensified to a kind of certainty, and if not a certainty of death, then at least of non-existence: the father and Bertrand had left this life, and if he shared the guilt for this death, everything remained in quiet apathy, and he didn't even have to consider whether it was Elisabeth or Ruzena he had stolen from Bertrand."

6. "He did not object when his father rummaged through his mail, and when it was given to him with the words: 'Unfortunately there seems to be still no news from your friend; [I wonder] whether he's coming at all,' Joachim wanted to hear only regret in this, despite the fact that it sounded to him like malice."

7. "Ruzena, after all, I'm a bad person and your enemy."

8. "Nevertheless the rumor persisted stubbornly that the old man through some kind of manipulation with the mail had destroyed the marriage and the fortune of his son."

9. *Briefe*, p.21.

10. "Nevertheless, after about eighteen months they had their first child. It just happened. How this came about need not be told. According to the material already presented on character development the reader can figure it out for himself."

11. "The Pastor entered and Bertrand was introduced as a friend of Joachim. 'Yes, the one comes, the other goes,' Herr v. Pasenow said thoughtfully, and those present didn't know whether this allusion to poor Helmuth was supposed to be a friendly gesture or a nasty crack at Bertrand."

12. " 'We are different from him,' she answered. Joachim was moved that she had said 'we.' 'He is perhaps uprooted,' he said, 'and perhaps he yearns to return.' Elizabeth said: 'Everyone is closed within himself.'—'But didn't we get the better part of it?' Joachim asked. . . . 'for he lives for business and he has to be cold and unfeeling. Think of your parents, of the words of your father. But he calls it

convention; he lacks true inwardness and Christianity.' He fell silent: O, what he had said hadn't been genuine."

13. " 'Yes, he was a blond, quiet boy, very reserved . . . he couldn't have changed much later, either.' "

14. " ' . . . anyway he was like you.' "

15. "That was too familiar, it almost seemed as though Bertrand wanted to use Helmuth's death for himself."

16. "Anyway it was no wonder that Bertrand remembered all the events of his earlier military career in such astonishing detail; one likes to recall better times which one has lost."

17. "These weeks were pregnant with misfortune and yet a good time; never, neither earlier nor later, had he been so close to his brother. Then came the misfortune with the pony. . . . there was a strict prohibition against riding on the fields on ground like this. But Joachim felt the greater privilege of one departing. . . . He had only started out with a short gallop when the misfortune already occurred; the pony stepped with its foreleg into a deep ditch, fell over, and couldn't stand up. . . . Joachim saw how he and Helmuth kneeled there and stroked the head of the animal, but he couldn't remember going home . . . then he had heard the voice of the mother: 'We have to tell father,' . . . Finally his father fastened the monocle in his eye: 'It is high time you left the house,' . . . then he saw how his father took the pistol from the case. Yes, and then he vomited. The next day he learned from the physician that he had suffered a concussion . . . it was again a good time, strangely secure and distant from all people. Nevertheless it ended and he was delivered to Culm a few weeks late . . . there seemed almost as though he had taken that feeling of distance along with him, and this made the adjustment there more tolerable for the time being."

18. "The characteristic of monumental art is not fullness of symbolism, but rather the essential symbol, the symbol that in a single image, a single event embraces and summarizes the fate of a whole and thus of all its members." ("Hofmannsthal und seine Zeit," in *Gesammelte Werke*, vol. 6, pp. 63 – 64). For a general discussion of Broch's "symbol theory" cf. Manfred Durzak, "Hermann Brochs Symboltheorie," *Neophilologus* 52 (1968): 156 – 169.

19. Broch knew Jung personally, but in 1932 still regarded him as a brilliant "Einzelgänger" without the prospect of developing a school. (Hermann Broch—Daniel Brody, *Briefwechsel 1930 – 1951*, ed. Bertold Hack and Marietta Kleiss [Frankfurt a/m: Buchhändler-Vereinigung, 1971], p.246).

20. "Above we saw that libido had to be sacrificed to the mother in order to create the world. Here the world is relinquished through the renewed sacrifice of the same libido, which belonged at first to the mother. The horse, therefore, can easily be substituted as a symbol for this libido with its many connections, as we have seen, to the mother. By the sacrifice of the horse, then, only a condition of introversion can be created, resembling the state prior to the creation of the world" (Carl Gustav Jung, *Wandlungen und Symbole der Libido: Beiträge zur Entwicklungsgeschichte des Denkens* [Leipzig and Vienna: Franz Deuticke, 1938], p.398).

21. "As Deussen comments, the sacrifice of the horse represents a renunciation of the universe. When the horse is sacrificed, in a certain sense the world is sacrificed and destroyed" (Idem.).

22. "Another symbol form is to be considered: At times the devil rides on a three-legged horse. The death-goddess Hel also rides in times of pestilence on a three-legged horse" (Ibid., p.273).

23. " . . . in order to thrust a cane through the legs of someone who walked like that, to bring him down somehow, to break his legs, to destroy that walk forever."

24. "Thus legs and cane go along together, and now the idea arises that the man would have become an ambler if he had been born a horse, but the most frightening and disgusting thing was that it is a three-legged amble . . . the devil strolls that way, a dog limping on three legs."

25. The expression "Schlafwandel" (as a metaphorical description of the behavior of a patient) appears in Freud's *Bemerkungen über einen Fall von Zwangsneurose* in a context that also contains, within three pages, a "wegwerfende Handbewegung" (cf. Bertrand's habit) and a lieutenant's urge to return money (cf. Pasenow's urge to return to his father the money the latter gives Ruzena). This motif first appears in Broch's work in 1909, shortly after the appearance of Freud's essay (cf. Manfred Durzak, *Hermann Broch* [Sammlung Metzler. Realienbücher für Germanisten. Abteilung Literaturgeschichte, M 58; Stuttgart: J. B. Metzlersche Verlagsbuchhandlung, 1967], p.13). All of this is not likely an accident, as I have argued elsewhere. But Heinz D. Osterle devoted a lengthy article to tracing the history of the term "sleepwalking," and concluded that Broch had derived the concept from Nietzsche on the strength of its association with the dance in the works of both writers ("Hermann Broch: 'Die Schlafwandler'. Kritik der zentralen Metapher," *Deutsche Vierteljahresschrift für Literaturwissenschaft und Geistesgeschichte* 44 (2) [1970]: 229–68). Cf. also Hartmut Steinecke, *Hermann Broch und der polyhistorische Roman* (Bonner Arbeiten zur deutschen Literatur, 17; Bonn: Bouvier Verlag, 1968), pp.138–55, for a discussion of the significance of the motif. Also Leo Kreutzer, *Erkenntnistheorie und Prophetie. Hermann Brochs Romantrilogie "Die Schlafwandler"* (Studien zur deutschen Literatur, 3; Tübingen: Max Niemeyer, 1966). pp.193–204.

26. Durzak, *Hermann Broch (op.cit.)*, p.18.

27. "The grape vines on the fences of the front gardens were red . . . and the horses in front of the four carriages at the street corner had sadly and peacefully bent forelegs."

28. "Now the child has arrived in an unfamiliar village, stumbles through silent streets in which here and there stand vehicles without horses."

29. "Esch didn't listen to him, but with an expression of ill temper and grief walked back and forth in the room with heavy awkward steps incommensurate with his gaunt frame. The swept floor creaked under the heavy step, and Huguenau looked at the holes and the powdered mortar between the planks, as well as Mr. Esch's heavy black shoes, which strangely enough were fastened not with shoelaces, but with a buckle that resembled part of a saddle."

30. " . . . that a sarcastic-ironic feature would show up in one of them had not been foreseeable. But whether this was determined by blood lines or was simply a freak of nature, or something that demonstrates the completion of a process in the descendant and frees him from all his forbears—this is difficult to say and a detail that interests no one, least of all Huguenau himself."

31. *Briefe*, p.21.

32. "Somewhere it didn't depend on individuals any more, they were all the same, and it didn't matter if one merged with the other and one sat in the place of the other."

33. " 'The dead were proper, too; to be sure, what this propriety really is can be seen in the legacy they've left behind.' 'What are you talking about?' 'Nothing, I was just thinking.' "

34. "When the epic ties Parikshit's birth and awakening to the celebration of the sacrifice of the horse, this is done for the purpose of bringing directly together times and men separated by a wide gulf." (Johann Jakob Bachofen, *Gesammelte Werke*, ed. Karl Meuli, 8 vols. [Basel: Benno Schwabe und Co. Verlag, 1943–1966], 8:89).

35. "For even Nuchem and Marie are strangers to me, they, on whom I had placed my final hope, the hope that I had taken their fate into my hands to determine it. Nuchem and Marie, they aren't my creation and never were. Deceptive hope, to be permitted to form the world!"

36. "But the two of them stood there with hanging arms, not daring to hold one another, not daring to dance, they stood there smiling stupidly."

37. "I have followed many paths to find the One into whom all others flow, but they led ever farther apart, and even God was not determined by me but by the fathers."

38. "I said to myself: 'You are a fool, you are a Platonist, you think by comprehending the world you can create it for yourself and find salvation into God. Haven't you noticed that you are bleeding to death?' "

39. In a passage Broch designated as the "menschlichen Kern des Ganzen" (*Briefe*, p.270), Virgil and Augustus argue in a friendly and nostalgic way over the color of the fetlocks of a horse they had raised together in their youth (pp.432–33). This incident, with its focus on the healthy leg of the horse, provides Virgil with the insight that he can leave the *Aneid* to Augustus as an act of friendship and of love, and die with this last worldly problem resolved. That Broch intended this focus on the horse's leg as a symbol of healthy libido is confirmed in a later passage in the novel: ". . . und tief im Westen, abschiedsgewärtiger als alle die anderen, ruhte das pegasische Ross quellschlagenden Hufes, . . . " (p.502).

40. Broch corresponded with Karl Kerényi and followed his activities and work fairly closely in the forties (Broch-Brody *Briefwechsel*, *op.cit.*, pp.483,485,504). For a letter of Kerényi to Broch cf. *Briefe (Gesammelte Werke*, vol. 8), p.277. For a brief discussion of the mythical function of Lysanias and Broch's assertion to Curt von Faber du Faur that he was totally unaware of Kerényi's writings on this figure of the child cf. Claudia Bernardoni, *Hermann Brochs "Tod des Vergil." Eine Interpretation auf Grund der theoretischen Schriften* (Ph.D. diss., Marburg Lahn, 1968), pp. 66–71, 218–19.

41. C. G. Jung and Karl Kerényi, *Das göttliche Kind* (Albae Vigiliae, 6 7; n.p.: Pantheon Akademische Verlagsanstalt, 1940). The first recognition of this work as a likely source for Broch is that of Curt von Faber du Faur: "Der Seelenführer in Herman Brochs 'Tod des Vergil'," in *Hermann Broch: Perspektiven der Forschung*, ed. Manfred Durzak (Munich: Wilhelm Fink, 1972), pp. 177–92 (the article was first published in 1957).

42. " 'Always you have searched for yourself and found me, and finding yourself you have sought me' " (*Der Tod des Vergil [Gesammelte Werke*, vol. 3], pp.292 f.

43. " . . . the torch was extinguished and cold in his hands—he roughhoused cheerfully with the others as though there were nothing in the world besides this game . . . And look, Lysanias gave no more answers at all; he just glanced up briefly as though he had a stranger in front of him, and then immediately turned back to his game."

44. "It is a striking paradox in all child myths that on the one hand the 'child' is exposed helplessly to overpowering enemies and threatened constantly with extinction, and on the other hand he has access to powers which far exceed normal human proportions. This assertion is closely tied to the psychological fact that the 'child' on the one hand is 'nondescript,' that is, unrecognized, 'only a child,' but on the other hand is god-like" (*Das göttliche Kind*, *op.cit.*, p.110).

45. "He recognized Lysanias in Plotia, and he was Lysanias himself, he recognized the slave in Lysanias, and he was the slave himself."

46. "In this *Coniunctio* a hermaphroditic light-form arises which is soon completed by the addition of the slave and the ego-personality of the poet. Only in this fourfold

unity does the wholeness of the person arise, embracing both consciousness and the unconscious" (Aniela Jaffe, "Hermann Broch: 'Der Tod des Vergil': Ein Beitrag zum Problem der Individuation," *Studien zur analytischen Psychologie C. G. Jungs* [Zurich: Rascher Verlag, 1955], pp.288–343).

47. " . . . for the fat one . . . advanced . . . lustfully pleading with outstretched hands, to reach the woman, who retreated scolding and swearing . . . he was fixed deaf and dumb upon his goal and certainly was not about to turn aside, if a surprising cane blow from the one who had quietly limped over had not suddenly ended the game: the fat one simply collapsed, rolled a little and remained quietly lying there— the murderer, however, paid no more attention to him."

48. " . . . then the fallen one roused himself, and after managing to turn onto his stomach he crawled on all fours like an animal, like a great fat beetle . . . hurriedly after his companions. Not comedy, no, fright and horror surrounded the fable animal."

49. In a dissertation that came to my attention too late to be included in this discussion, Irmgard Kahle has discussed "myth and poeisis" in *Der Tod des Vergil*, including (according to a review in *Germanistik*) some reference to my original treatment of the split self in Broch's work (cf. Preface, n. 1, above). (*Anfang und Kindheit. Die Korrelate von Mythos und Poiesis in Hermann Brochs "Tod des Vergil* [Ph.D. diss., Aachen, 1976]).

Works Cited

Preface

Waldeck, Peter B. *Die Kindheitsproblematik bei Hermann Broch*. Munich: Wilhelm Fink Verlag, 1968.

Introduction

Freud, Sigmund. "Der Dichter und das Phantasieren." In *Gesammelte Werke*, vol 7, edited by Anna Freud et al. Frankfurt am Main: S. Fischer, 1941.

Jung, Carl Gustav, and Kerényi, Karl. *Das göttliche Kind*. Albae Vigiliae, 6/7. N.p.: Pantheon Akademische Verlagsanstalt, 1940.

Keppler, Carl. *The Literature of the Second Self*. Tucson: University of Arizona Press, 1972.

Rogers, Robert. *A Psychoanalytic Study of the Double in Literature*. Detroit, Mich.: Wayne State University Press, 1970.

Wain, Marianne. "The Double in Romantic Narrative: A Preliminary Study." *Germanic Review* 36(4) (December, 1961): 258–68.

Introduction to Part 1

Gräf, H. A. *Goethe über seine Dichtungen*. *Drama III*. Frankfurt am Main: Rütter und Loening, 1906.

Korff, H. A. *Geist der Goethezeit*. 3 vols. Leipzig: J. J. Weber, 1923.

Chapter 1: Goetz von Berlichingen and the Young Goethe

Goethe, Johann Wolfgang von. *Goethes Werke*. 14 vols. Edited by Erich Trunz. Hamburg: Christian Wegner Verlag, 1948-.

⸻. *Goethe. Götz von Berlichingen*. Edited by Jutta Neuendorff-Fürstenau. Berlin: Akademie Verlag, 1958.

Graham, Ilse A. *Goethe and Lessing: The Wellsprings of Creation*. London: Elek Books, 1973.

⸻. "Vom *Urgötz* zum *Götz*: Neufassung oder Neuschöpfung?" *Jahrbuch der deutschen Schillergesellschaft* 9 (1965): 245–82.

Herder, Johann Gottfried. "Shakespeare." In *Sturm und Drang: Kritische Schriften*. Heidelberg: Verlag Lambert Schneider, 1963, pp. 555–78.

Martini, Fritz. "Goethe's *Götz von Berlichingen*: Charakterdrama und Gesellschaftsdrama." In *Dichten und Lesen*, edited by Ferdinand van Ingen et al. Utrechese Publikaties voor algemene Literatuurwetenschap. Groningen: Wolters-Noordhoff, 1972.

Meyer, Heinrich. *Goethe: Das Leben im Werk*. Hamburg-Bergedorf: Stromverlag, 1949.

Chapter 2: J. M. R. Lenz: *Der Hofmeister*

Applebaum-Graham, Ilse. "The Currency of Love: A Reading of Lessing's *Minna von Barnhelm*." *German Life and Letters* 18 (1964): 270–78.

Arntzen, Helmut. *Die ernste Komödie: Das deutsche Lustspiel von Lessing bis Kleist*. Sammlung Dialog. Munich: Nymphenburger Verlagshandlung, 1968.

Burger, Heinz Otto. "J. M. R. Lenz: *Der Hofmeister*." In *Das deutsche Lustspiel*, vol. 1, edited by Hans Steffen. Kleine Vandenhoeck Reihe, no. 271S. Göttingen: Vandenhoeck und Ruprecht, 1968, pp. 48–67.

Girard, Rene. *Lenz 1751-1792: Genese d'une dramaturgie du Tragi comique*. Paris: Librarie C. Klincksieck, 1968.

Guthke, Karl S. "Nachwort" to J. M. R. Lenz: *Der Hofmeister*. Universalbibliothek, no. 1376. Stuttgart: Reclam Verlag, 1966.

Harris, Edward P. "Structural Unity in J. M. R. Lenz's *Der Hofmeister*: A Revaluation." *Seminar* 8 (1972): 77–87.

Jung, Carl Gustav. *Psychologie und Alchemie*. Zurich: Rascher Verlag, 1944.

Leisewitz, J. A. *Julius von Tarent*. In *Sturm und Drang: Dramatische Schriften*, 2 vols, edited by Erich Loewenthal and Lambert Schneider. Heidelberg: Verlag Lambert Schneider, n.d., 1:555–614.

Lenz, J. M. R. *Anmerkungen übers Theater*. In *Sturm und Drang: Kritische Schriften*. Heidelberg: Verlag Lambert Schneider, 1963, pp. 715–46.

———. *Gesammelte Werke in vier Bänden*. Edited by Richard Daunicht. Munich: Wilhelm Fink, 1967.

————. *Werke und Schriften*. 2 vols. Edited by Britta Titel and Helmut Haug. Stuttgart: Govert, 1966.

Rieger, Max. *Klinger in der Sturm- und Drangperiode*. Darmstadt: Arnold Bergstrasser, 1880.

Schöne, Albrecht. *Säkularisation als sprachbildende Kraft*. Studien zur Dichtung deutscher Pfarrersöhne, Palaestra, no. 226. Göttingen: Vandenhoeck und Ruprecht, 1958.

Chapter 3: F. M. Klinger: *Die Zwillinge*

Guthke, Karl S. "F. M. Klingers *Zwillinge:* Höhepunkt und Krise des Sturm und Drang." *German Quarterly* 43(4) November 1970): 703–14.

Hering, Christoph. *Friedrich Maximilian Klinger: Der Weltmann als Dichter*. Berlin: DeGruyter, 1966.

Klinger, Friedrich Maximilian. *Der Weltmann und der Dichter*. In *F. M. Klingers Sämmtliche Werke*, vol. 9. Stuttgart and Tübingen: J. G. Cotta'scher Verlag, 1842.

————. *Dramatische Jugendwerke*. 3 vols. Edited by Hans Berendt and Kurt Wolff. Leipzig: Ernst Rowohlt, 1912.

Kolb, Luise. *Klingers "Simsone Grisaldo"*. Ph.D. dissertation, Halle, 1929.

Mattenklott, Gert. *Melancholie in der Dramatik des Sturm und Drang*. Studien zur allgemeinen und vergleichenden Literaturwissenschaft, 1. Stuttgart: J. B. Metzlersche Verlagshandlung, 1968.

Palitsche, Otto A. *Erlebnisgehalt und Formproblem in Friedrich Maximilian Klingers Jugenddramen*. Hamburgische Texte und Untersuchungen zur deutschen Philologie, II,2. Dortmund: Ruhfus, 1924.

Rieger, Max. *Klinger in der Sturm- und Drangperiode*. Darmstadt: Arnold Bergstrasser, 1880.

Schmidt, Erich. *Lenz und Klinger: Zwei Dichter der Geniezeit.* Berlin: Weidemann, 1878.

Waidson, H. M. "Goethe and Klinger: Some Aspects of a Personal and Literary Relationship." *English Goethe Society Publications,* n.s. 23 (1953/54): 97–120.

Wiget, Wilhelm. "Einleitung" to *Eine Unbekannte Fassung von Klingers Zwillingen.* Acta et commentationes, B 28. Tartu: K. Mattienseni, 1932.

Wyneken,Friedrich. *Rousseaus Einfluß auf Klinger.* University of California Publications in Modern Philology, III, 1. Berkeley: University of California, 1912.

Chapter 4: Friedrich Schiller: *Die Räuber*

Ermatinger, Emil. *Deutsche Dichter 1700-1900. Zweiter Teil.* Bonn: Athenäum Verlag, 1949.

Graham, Ilse A. *Schiller's Drama: Talent and Integrity.* London: Methuen, 1974.

Heyn, Gisa. *Der junge Schiller als Psychologe.* Zurich: Juris Verlag, 1966.

Jonas, Fritz. *Schillers Briefe.* 7 vols. Stuttgart; Berlin, Leipzig: Deutsche Verlagsanstalt, 1892-96.

Keller, Alfred. *Die literarischen Beziehungen zwischen den Erstlingsdramen Klingers und Schillers.* Ph.D. dissertation, Bern, 1911.

Lecke, Bodo, ed. *Friedrich Schiller. Von den Anfängen bis 1795.* Dichter über ihre Dichtungen. Munich: Heimeran, 1969.

Martini, Fritz. "Die feindlichen Brüder. Zum Problem des gesellschaftskritischen Dramas von J. A. Leisewitz, F. M. Klinger und F. Schiller." *Jahrbuch der deutschen Schillergesellschaft* 16 (1972): 208 –65.

Masson, R. "Un ancêtre de Franz Moor." *Etudes Germaniques* 25(1) (1970): 1–6.

Michelsen, Peter. "Studien zu Schillers *Räubern.*" *Jahrbuch der deutschen Schillergesellschaft* 8 (1964): 57–111.

Münch, Else. "Schillers *Räuber* und Klingers *Zwillinge.*" *Zeitschrift für Deutschkunde* 10 (1932): 710–21.

Robertson, John G. *Schiller After a Century.* Edinburgh and London: William Blackwood and Sons, 1905.

Schiller, Johann Christoph Friedrich. *Die Braut von Messina.* Vol. 2 of *Sämtliche Werke,* edited by Gerhard Fricke and Herbert G. Göpfert. Munich: Carl Hanser, 1959.

————. *Die Räuber.* Vol. 3 of *Schillers Werke* (Nationalausgabe), edited by Herbert Stubenrauch. Weimar: H. Böhlaus Nachfolger, 1953.

Schubart, Christian Daniel. *Schubarts Werke in einem Band.* Edited by Ursula Wertheim and Hans Böhm. Weimar: Volksverlag, 1959.

Storz, Gerhart. *Der Dichter Friedrich Schiller.* Stuttgart: Ernst Klett, 1959.

Veit, Philipp F. "The Strange Case of Moritz Spiegelberg." *Germanic Review* 44 (1969): 171–85.

von Wiese, Benno. *Friedrich Schiller.* Stuttgart: Metzler, 1963.

Chapter 5: Franz Grillparzer: "Der Arme Spielmann" and Die Jüdin von Toledo

Brinkmann, Richard. *Wirklichkeit und Illusion. Studien über Gehalt und Grenzen des Begriffs Realismus für die erzählende Dichtung des 19. Jahrhunderts.* Tübingen: Max Niemeyer, 1957, pp. 87–145.

Ellis, John M. *Narration in the German Novelle.* Angelica Germanica Series, 2. Cambridge: Cambridge University Press, 1974.

Frey-Staiger, Eleonore. *Grillparzer: Gestalt und Gestaltung des Traums*. Zürcher Beiträge zur deutschen Literatur-und Geistesgeschichte, 26. Zürich: Atlantis Verlag, 1966.

Grillparzer, Franz. *Sämtliche Werke*. Edited by Peter Frank and Karl Pörnbacher. Munich: Carl Hanser, 1964.

Jungbluth, Günther. "Franz Grillparzers Erzählung 'Der arme Spielmann'. Ein Beitrag zu ihrem Verstehen." *Orbis Litterarum* 24(9) (1969): 35–51.

Martini, Fritz. "Die treuen Diener ihrer Herrn. Zu F. M. Klinger und F. Grillparzer." *Jahrbuch der Grillparzer Gesellschaft* 12 (1976): 147–77.

Müller, Joachim. "Grillparzer und Goethe. Grillparzers Goetheverständnis und Goethe-Bild." *Chronik des Wiener Goethe-Vereins* 74 (1970): 30–57.

Paulsen, Wolfgang. *Die Ahnfrau. Zu Grillparzers früher Dramatik*. Tübingen: Max Niemeyer, 1962.

———. "Nachwort" to *Die Jüdin von Toledo*. Universalbibliothek, no. 4394. Stuttgart: Reclam, 1968.

Politzer, Heinz. Franz Grillparzers "Der arme Spielmann." Dichtung und Erkenntnis, 2. Stuttgart: Metzler, 1967.

Skreb, Zdenko. "Das Märchenspiel bei Grillparzer." *Jahrbuch der Grillparzer-Gesellschaft*, dritte Folge 7 (1967): 37–55.

von Roques-von Beit, Hedwig. *Symbolik des Märchens. Versuch einer Deutung*. 2 vols. Bern: Francke Verlag, 1960.

Chapter 6: Frank Wedekind: *Der Marquis von Keith* and Walter Hasenclever: *Der Sohn*

Hasenclever, Walter. *Der Sohn. Ein Drama in fünf Akten*. Berlin: Propyläen Verlag, 1917.

Kutscher, Artur. *Wedekind. Leben und Werk*. Edited by Karl Ude. Munich: List Verlag, 1964.

MacClean, H. "Wedekind's *Der Marquis von Keith:* An Interpretation Based on the Faust and Circus Motifs." *Germanic Review* 43 (1968): 164–87.

Paulsen, Wolfgang. "Walter Hasenclever." In *Expressionismus als Literatur. Gesammelte Studien.* Edited by Wolfgang Rothe. Bern and Munich: Francke Verlag, 1969.

Raggam, Miriam. *Walter Hasenclever. Leben und Werk.* Hildesheim: Verlag Dr. H. A. Gerstenberg, 1973.

Sachs, Hans. "Der Sohn." *Imago* (1919), pp. 43–48.

Wedekind, Frank. *Gesammelte Werke.* 9 vols. Munich: Georg Müller, 1924.

Chapter 7: Franz Kafka: *"Das Urteil"*

Beck, Evelyn T. *Kafka and the Yiddish Theater: A Study of the Impact of the Yiddish Theater on the Work of Franz Kafka.* Ph.D. dissertation, University of Wisconsin, 1970.

Beicken, Peter U. *Franz Kafka: Eine kritische Einführung in die Forschung.* Frankfurt am Main: Athenaion Verlag, 1974.

Brod, Max. *Franz Kafka: Eine Biographie.* Fischer Bücherei, 552. Frankfurt am Main: Fischer Verlag, 1966.

Jung, Carl Gustav. *Wandlungen and Symbole der Libido: Beiträge zur Entwicklungsgeschichte des Denkens.* 3rd ed. Vienna and Leipzig: Franz Deuticke, 1938.

Kafka, Franz. *Die Beschreibung eines Kampfes.* Vol. 5 of *Gesammelte Schriften,* edited by Max Brod. New York: Schocken Books, 1946.

———. *Briefe an Felice.* Edited by Erich Heller and Jürgen Born. Frankfurt am Main: Schocken Verlag, 1967.

———. *Erzählungen.* 3d ed. New York: Schocken Books, 1946.

———. *Das Schloß.* n.p.: S. Fischer Verlag, 1958.

————. *Tagebücher 1910-1923*. Edited by Max Brod. New York: Schocken Books, 1948/49.

Laing, R. D. *The Divided Self*. New York: Pantheon Books, 1969.

Politzer, Heinz. *Franz Kafka: Der Künstler*. Frankfurt am Main: S. Fischer Verlag, 1965.

Pondrom, Cyrena N. "Coherence in Kafka's 'The Judgment': Georg's Perceptions of the World." *Studies in Short Fiction* 9 (1972): 59–79.

Seidler, Ingo. "Das Urteil: Freud natürlich? Zum Problem der Multivalenz bei Kafka." In *Psychologie in der Literaturwissenschaft. Viertes Amherster Kolloquium zur modernen deutschen Literatur*, edited by Wolfgang Paulsen. Heidelberg: Lothar Stiehm Verlag, 1971, pp. 174–90.

Sokel, Walter. *Franz Kafka: Tragik und Ironie*. Munich and Vienna: Albert Langen Georg Müller Verlag, 1964.

Weber, Albrecht. "Das Urteil." In Albrecht Weber, Carsten Schlingmann, and Gert Kleinschmidt, *Interpretationen zu Franz Kafka*. Munich: R. Oldenbourg Verlag, 1968, pp. 9–80.

Chapter 8: Hermann Broch: *Die Schlafwandler*

Bachofen, Johann Jakob. *Gesammelte Werke*. 8 vols. Edited by Karl Meuli. Basel: Benno Schwabe & Co. Verlag, 1943-1966.

Bernardoni, Claudia. *Hermann Brochs "Tod des Vergil": Eine Interpretation auf Grund der theoretischen Schriften*. Ph.D. dissertation, Marburg/Lahn, 1968.

Broch, Hermann. *Gesammelte Werke*. 10 vols. Zurich: Rhein-Verlag, 1953-1961.

Broch, Hermann, and Brody, Daniel. *Briefwechsel 1930-1951*. Edited by Bertold Hack and Marietta Kleiss. Frankfurt am Main: Buchhändler-Vereinigung, 1971.

Durzak, Manfred. *Hermann Broch.* Sammlung Metzler. Realien-bücher für Germanisten. Abteilung Literaturgeschichte, M 58. Stuttgart: J. B. Metzlersche Verlagsbuchhandlung, 1967.

————. "Hermann Brochs Symboltheorie." *Neophilologus* 52 (1968): 156–69.

————, ed. *Hermann Broch: Perspektiven der Forschung.* Munich: Wilhelm Fink Verlag, 1972.

Jaffe, Aniela. "Hermann Broch: 'Der Tod des Vergil': Ein Beitrag zum Problem der Individuation." In *Studien zur analytischen Psychologie C. G. Jungs.* Zurich: Rascher Verlag, 1955, pp. 288–343.

Kahle, Irmgard. *Anfang und Kindheit. Die Korrelate von Mythos und Poiesis in Hermann Brochs "Tod des Vergil."* Ph.D. dissertation, Aachen, 1976.

Kreutzer, Leo. *Erkenntnishtheorie und Prophetie: Hermann Brochs Romantrilogie "Die Schlafwandler."* Studien zur deutschen Literatur, 3. Tübingen: Max Niemeyer, 1966.

Osterle, Heinz D. "Hermann Broch: 'Die Schlafwandler'. Kritik der zentralen Metapher," *Deutsche Vierteljahresschrift für Literaturwissenschaft und Geistesgeschichte* 44 (2) (1970): 229–68.

————. "*Die Schlafwandler:* Revolution und Apokalypse," *PMLA* 86(5) (October, 1971): 946–58.

Steinecke, Hartmut. *Hermann Broch und der polyhistorische Roman.* Bonner Arbeiten zur deutschen Literatur, 17. Bonn: Bouvier Verlag, 1968.

Index